D1608835

POMPEII · AD 79

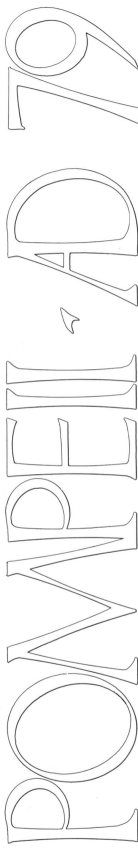

*The Eruption of Vesuvius and the
Death of Pliny*
A PAINTING BY
PIERRE–HENRI DE VALENCIENNES
1813, FROM MUSÉE DES AUGUSTINS,
TOULOUSE, FRANCE

The Treasure of Rediscovery

Text by RICHARD BRILLIANT

An official publication of The American Museum of Natural History, New York

Clarkson N. Potter, Inc./Publishers NEW YORK
DISTRIBUTED BY CROWN PUBLISHERS, INC.

ON THE PRECEDING PAGE:

*The mosaic frieze of theater masks on which the title
is superimposed—an artistic interpretation painted by
Wilhelm Zahn in 1850—was originally a doorsill
between the entry corridor and the atrium in the
House of the Faun. The mask to the left, a part of this
frieze, typifies those worn in the tragedies performed in
Pompeii.*

x

Contents

The four glass receptacles shown, while actually colorless, appear to have a translucent tint. Glass was commonly used for beakers, amphorae and glasses in Pompeii where these vessels were found.

Acknowledgments

THIS book was undertaken shortly after my own house burned down during a severe electrical storm on May 31, 1978. The suddenness of the event, the destruction of possessions and shelter, the challenge to my sense of security and privacy in the midst of the storm made me especially receptive to the greater dilemma and tragedy of Pompeii and the Pompeians so long ago, and yet so immediate. The ruin of my house and the dislocation of my library also made me depend on the assistance of others for the completion of this memoir of Pompeii. It could not have been written without them, and I wish to thank them most warmly for their timely and reliable research: Bettina Bergmann on the effect of Pompeii on central European art and literature and the role of German archaeologists and classicists; David Friedman on Pompeii in France and England to the late nineteenth century and on Neoclassicism; and Susan Wood on the history of Pompeian archaeology from 1748 to 1975.

In addition, the resourceful and energetic work of Kay Zakariasen in assembling the visual material for the book has done exemplary justice to the ancient town. She was greatly aided in her efforts by members of the American Academy in Rome, Professor John D'Arms, the Director, and Professor Ann Laidlaw, "Pompeianist," and by those distinguished Italian archaeologists who are intimately associated with the excavations at Pompeii: Professore Alfonso de Franciscis, the former Director; Dottore Fausto Zevi, Soprintendente alle Antichità (Naples); and Dottoressa Giuseppina Cerulli-Irelli, current Director at Pompeii.

This book is dedicated to my mother, Pauline Apt Brilliant—faithful to tradition.

RICHARD BRILLIANT
November 25, 1978

*Alabaster relief of a lobster combined with a typical sacred landscape,
showing the wall of a shrine—possibly to Priapus (from a private collection,
Werner Forman Archive).*

POMPEII · AD 79

Step now with greater care:
At a stone's throw from here
A far rarer scene
Is being prepared for your gaze.
The door of a little temple,
Rusted, is closed for ever.
A great light lies
Down on the grassy threshold
Here will never resound
Men's steps again, or a mourning feigned and
     cold.
Only a lean dog watches, stretched on the ground.
He will not stir, not stir
All through this hour that stares with sultry face.
Above the roof a kingly
Cloud looks out to space.[1]

—EUGENIO MONTALE

2

Disaster
August 24, A.D. 79

PICTURE for yourself an ancient town, Pompeii, set in fertile Campania between Mount Vesuvius and the sea, its some 20,000 inhabitants perhaps less active than usual because of the midsummer heat. The density of occupation only exacerbated the temperature because this population was crowded into an area of little more than 36 acres (64 hectares), surrounded by the constraint of the old defensive wall, almost two miles in length (3 kilometers), which together with the narrow streets hindered the freshening circulation of air. Of course, these same narrow streets did provide protection against the sun, as did the porticos of the Forum, but most Pompeians found refuge in the shadowy interiors of their houses, in the privacy of their own gardens, or forgot the heat in the pursuit of pleasure or profit.

*Fast food, First Century style. A curbside customer waits in anticipation
as one of the thermopolium vats is replenished. Shady shelter is supplied
by the hanging balcony, while the serpent and Mercury painted on the building
wall provide protection (and hopefully good fortune) to all passersby.*

Crude rendition of the brawl between the Nucerians and Pompeians at the Amphitheater in A.D. 59. Combatants can be seen on the steps, seats and the floor of the arena, but we also get a view of the encircling area including trees, open-air refreshment stalls, and the carrying litters used by the affluent as transport to and from the gladiatorial contests.

Numerous public buildings crowded around the Forum, dedicated to the business of government (the flanking *Halls of the Duoviri*, of the *Aediles*, and of the *Town Council*, together with the nearby *Comitium* or meeting place of the citizenry), to the exercise of the official cults (*Temples of Apollo, Jupiter*, the *Emperor Vespasian*, the *Sanctuary of the Lares*), to the corporate headquarters of the Fullers "guild" located in the *Building of Eumachia*, and to the purchase of foodstuffs in the provision market or *Macellum*. These institutionalized functions drew many people to the Forum, especially down the principal commercial street of Pompeii, the *Via dell'Abbondanza*, which was lined for the most part by houses whose street frontage was given over to commercial exploitation by various shopkeepers, purveyors of hot food and wine, and artisans. Traffic on this street was heavy, witness the abundant signs and political slogans painted on the façades, but it was not only the commercial development of the street that drew the crowds. The Via dell'Abbondanza ran slightly north of the two main centers of public entertainment, the large area containing the *Amphitheater* and the *Large Palaestra* between the *Sarno* and *Nucerian Gates*, and the smaller, more developed zone to the west of the *Stabian Gate*, dominated by the *Large Theater*. The amphitheater itself held almost the entire population, but probably also attracted to its gladiatorial contests and races spectators from some of the surrounding towns who may have come to enjoy the many wineshops and bars of Pompeii (118 in number), its restaurants and brothels, its public baths, especially on market day which occurred every eight days. These gladiatorial shows in the amphitheater could become raucous and even violent affairs, as in A.D. 59 when a destructive riot broke out in the amphitheater between the Pompeians and their visitors from nearby Nuceria and many were killed or injured; the Roman Senate barred such shows for the next ten years, but politics under Nero and his own love of the games probably cut short the interdict (see Tacitus, *Annals* XIV.17).

The presence of the Nucerians at the Pompeian amphitheater suggests that the abundant entertainments available in Pompeii were not intended for local consumption alone, even if the townspeople had an epicurean taste for pleasure, but formed an industry that brought wealth to Pompeii from the surrounding region. There were other ways to milk the traffic brought to the games in the amphitheater. Set advantageously on the Via dell'Abbondanza next to the amphitheater was the *Villa* or *Praedia of Julia Felix* which occupied a double lot. Julia Felix rented bathing facilities to

Spectators ogle the spectacle in the Small Theater (Odeon). Performing in the band are several players with auloi (ancient Greek double pipes with oboe reeds) while the female leader brandishes a baton to the choral accompaniment.

*Standing and kneeling worshipers gather in the forecourt of the Temple of
Fortune while smoke rises in aromatic tendrils from the incense burner.*

the "right people," stores with flats above, and first-floor apartments for five-year leases, beginning August 1. Julia was, also, a resident landlady and kept for herself the best part of the property, including a magnificent garden. In this respect she anticipated the noble proprietors of Renaissance Rome.

If the amphitheater pandered to the more violent emotions, the performances in the *Large Theater*, located near the *Stabian Gate*, probably offered a mixed bill of plays, burlesque sketches, and comic playlets, with the Latin classics of Plautus and Terence less frequently presented than watered-down versions of Greek works, especially by Euripides, and the very popular repertory of antiheroic skits and scatological sketches, long known and esteemed in southern Italy. Several thousands might attend the performances in the Theater, but perhaps only a thousand spectators could be seated in the neighboring *Odeon*, a small covered theater, suitable for concerts, the dance, and pantomimes, where possibly the audience had greater cultural ambitions. Behind the Theater a large rectangular, porticated courtyard opened up, a typical arrangement in Roman theater-complexes, because the *Quadriporticus* gave ample room to the spectators of the Theater when they wished to circulate during intermissions in the performances. The Porticus behind the Large Theater may also have served as a *School for Gladiators*, at least in part, although by A.D. 62 the quadriporticus had been transformed into *Gladiatorial Barracks*. If not the games in the amphitheater after the riot of A.D. 59, at least the Pompeians could admire the gladiators in training, and otherwise.

Activities in the theater district were further complicated and enriched by sacred presences: the old *Doric Temple* in the nearby *Triangular Forum*, probably dedicated to Hercules and Minerva, a *Temple of Jupiter Milichius*, and especially the *Temple of Isis*, the great Egyptian goddess who inspired the greatest fervor in her devotees. Yet, whatever may have been her strength among the faithful, Dionysus and Venus held greater popular sway in Pompeii, perhaps because they offered more for less. The cult of Dionysus was widely observed in dedications, votive objects, and in the full enjoyment of his bounty, the wine. The only known *Temple of Dionysus* lies outside of town to the south on the Hill of Sant'Abbondio, while the deepest passion of his religion informs the greatest of all religious paintings in Pompeii, held secret in the *Villa of the Mysteries*, also out of town to the northwest on the Herculaneum Road. Most popular of all was the cult of Venus, celebrated in her large *Temple*, placed on a high platform beside the *Marine Gate*, but most

Wall-painting embellishment to one of the lacquer-red walls in the House of Sallust exemplifies the rich and lavish decor preferred by wealthy Pompeians.

prominently in numerous dedicatory inscriptions and paintings which glorify her role as patron of love and mistress of all nature for the benefit of Pompeii. Popular religion rather than piety seemed preferable in a fruitful land.

Pompeii, indeed, may have owed its fair prosperity in part to its favorable environment, but even more to the industry of its citizens, to its merchants, storekeepers, and artisans and to the products for which the town was best known, woolen cloth and *garum*, a fish sauce widely used in Roman cooking as a condiment. Descendants of Greeks, Samnites, Oscans, and Roman veterans settled by Sulla after 80 B.C., provincial in manner and speech, the townspeople of Pompeii depended on a leadership group, formed largely of merchants and shopkeepers, an aristocracy of the middle. Even if some Pompeians had connections to Roman magnates as their clients or dependents and, thus, had limited access to the cultural, intellectual, and artistic movements of the day, there was no "big money" in town, no salon as could be found in neighboring Herculaneum, a small but elegant resort (in the *Villa of the Papyri*), and few if any celebrities. Therefore, it is most remarkable that these citizens of modest means not only commissioned a large number of public buildings, distinguished by their quality and costliness, but also erected fine houses for themselves and decorated them richly with painted walls and ceilings, mosaic floors, lavish furnishings, elaborate private gardens, pools of water and fountains, and everywhere works of art.

Significantly, the greatest attention was given to the embellishment of the houses, fortresses against the world, the private environment in which the worthier citizens lived the best part of their lives. Although the form of the Pompeian town house was never stable and from the third century B.C. on moved in the direction of greater complexity and away from symmetry and axiality, certain characteristics persevered. An opaque façade was offered to the street with few if any windows and limited openings, although even the most elegant house could provide commercial space on the street without any access to the interior. That dark, shadowy interior, filled with small rooms, was punctuated by rhythmic openings to light and air either through the roof (*atrium* and *peristyle*) or by the freshness of gardens and parks, wholly contained within the perimeter walls of the house; clearly such houses were better suited to warm weather than to the brief but chilly Campanian winter. Color was everywhere, decorating the opaque street façade and the complex interiors, the latter by extensive programs of

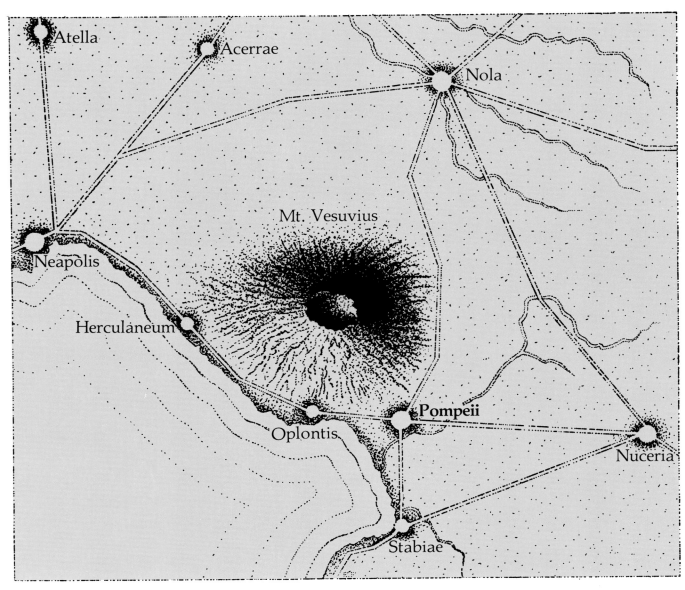

Map of the Crater of Vesuvius and the cities and towns in the immediate vicinity prior to the eruption in A.D. 79.

decoration consisting of ornamental schemes which organize wall, ceiling, and floor. Such schemes often set off prestigious collections of works of art in replica, borrowed from an acknowledged repertory of "masterpieces" of painting and sculpture, usually of Greek origin. Even when the houses are large (e.g. *House of the Faun, of Sallust, of Pansa* (Arriana Polliana), *of Menander, of the Tragic Poet, of Meleager, of the Dioscuri* (Castor and Pollux)) and occupy entire blocks, the rooms are small in scale, full of changes, and surprisingly intimate. Perhaps because of this and because the public spaces in town have no greenery, in some houses—*of the Vettii, of Loreius Tiburtinus* (now D. Octavius Quartio), *of Julia Felix*, and the *Villa of Diomedes* outside the Herculaneum Gate—the exterior/interior garden came to dominate the ensemble, as if the landscape had been brought indoors for the peaceful contemplation of the resident.

More modest houses were common, but the multistoried tenements that had already begun to develop in Rome, or in the port cities of Ostia and Puteoli (Pozzuoli), do not appear in Pompeii. For the poor and for the slaves, for everyone, public life was carried on in public places and in the streets, paved with blocks of stone and often equipped with sidewalks and stepping stones at the crosswalks. Public and private fountains abounded; water for human consumption, for private and public bathing was brought to Pompeii by an aqueduct which came down from Abellinum (Avellino) almost fifteen miles (26 kilometers) away.

Some problems intruded into this salubrious environment in the first century A.D. Pompeii's expansion westward toward the sea was blocked by *Stabiae* which controlled the coastal trade and fishing. To the east beyond Vesuvius, the towns along the inland route including *Capua, Nola*, and *Nuceria* prospered and apparently relied less on the market facilities offered by Pompeii, while the old wool trade suffered in competition with the developing provinces of the West. Furthermore, despite the continuing importance of the old Greek city *Neapolis* (Naples), the weight of commercial, industrial, and military activity in the Bay of Naples had shifted northward to concentrate on Puteoli and on the base at Misenum. Then, on February 5, A.D. 62, a

Relief depicting the destruction during the earthquake in A.D. 62: from left to right, the Triumphal Arch lists badly, the Temple of Jupiter flanked by two equestrian statues topples; then sharing equal billing with the calamity come the trappings of sacrificial offerings to appease the gods and protect against any repetition of the event (portrayed on the pedestal of the lararium in the home of Lucius Caecilius Jucundus).

major earthquake badly damaged the town, seriously affecting many of the public buildings in the Forum, several of the temples, and many of the private houses. Rebuilding was slow, although the decorators were busy making cosmetic alterations while introducing the new fashions into the damaged houses of Pompeii. About the 20th of August, A.D. 79 the earth tremors began again and continued for four days until the morning of the 24th when the world came to an end.

Fortunately for posterity this cataclysmic event of nature, the eruption of Mount Vesuvius, touched directly a distinguished Roman citizen, a man of letters, the Younger Pliny who was at Misenum visiting his uncle, the Elder Pliny. Himself a man of great erudition and the author of an encyclopedic work on natural history, the Elder Pliny was at that time commander of the naval base at Misenum. True to his sense of duty and despite his age, the Elder Pliny set out on a mission of exploration and rescue only to lose his life. Years later at the request of the great Roman historian, Tacitus, the Younger Pliny wrote two letters describing the violent and fatal events of this terrible day, probably intended as the basis of Tacitus' own historical treatment. That portion of Tacitus' history does not survive, but Pliny's letters do:

"*The exhalation alone was so thick and black, as to involve the country in darkness, while the noise and continued tremor excited universal terror. The cinders covered the transmarine provinces . . . poured with the force and impetus of mighty torrents, overwhelming the country to the tops of trees . . .*"

—CAMPI PHLEGRAEI

Thank you for asking me to send you a description of my uncle's death so that you can leave an accurate account of it for posterity; I know that immortal fame awaits him if his death is recorded by you. It is true that he perished in a catastrophe which destroyed the loveliest regions of the earth, a fate shared by whole cities and their people, and one so memorable that it is likely to make his name live for ever: and he himself wrote a number of books of lasting value: but you write for all time and can still do much to perpetuate his memory . . .

My uncle was stationed at Misenum, in active command of the fleet. On 24 August, in the early afternoon, my mother drew his attention to a cloud of unusual size and appearance. He had been out in the sun, had taken a cold bath, and lunched while lying down, and was then working at his books. He called for his shoes and climbed up to a place which would give him the best view of the phenomenon. It was not clear at that distance from which mountain the cloud was rising (it was afterwards known to be

"Fountains or jets of flame marked the commencement of the explosion, and issuing from a long rent in the side of the mountain, threw balls of fire in all directions. Volleys of thunder, with darkness and agitation, succeeded."

—Campi Phlegraei

Vesuvius); its general appearance can best be expressed as being like a [Mediterranean umbrella] pine rather than any other tree, for it rose to a great height on a sort of trunk and then split off into branches, I imagine because it was thrust upwards by the first blast and then left unsupported as the pressure subsided, or else it was borne down by its own weight so that it spread out and gradually dispersed. Sometimes it looked white, sometimes blotched and dirty, according to the amount of soil and ashes it carried with it. My uncle's scholarly acumen saw at once that it was important enough for a closer inspection, and he ordered a boat to be made ready, telling me I could come with him if I wished. I replied that I preferred to go on with my studies, and as it happened he had himself given me some writing to do.

As he was leaving the house he was handed a message from Rectina, wife of Tascus, whose house was at the foot of the mountain, so that escape was impossible except by boat. She was terrified by the danger threatening her and implored him to rescue her from her fate. He changed his plans, and what he had begun in a spirit of inquiry he completed as a hero. He gave orders for the warships to be launched and went on board himself with the intention of bringing help to many more people besides Rectina, for this lovely stretch of coast was thickly populated. He hurried to the place which everyone else was hastily leaving, steering his course straight for the danger zone. He was entirely fearless, describing each new movement and phase of the portent to be noted down exactly as he observed them. Ashes were already falling, hotter and thicker as the ships drew near, followed by bits of pumice and blackened stones, charred and cracked by the flames: then suddenly they were in shallow water, and the shore was blocked by the debris from the mountain. For a moment my uncle wondered whether to turn back, but when the helmsman advised this he refused, telling him that Fortune stood by the courageous and they must make for Pomponianus at Stabiae. He was cut off there by the breadth of the bay (for the shore gradually curves round a basin filled by the sea) so that he was not as yet in danger, though it was clear that this would come nearer as it spread. Pomponianus had therefore already put his belongings on board ship, intending to escape if the contrary wind fell. This wind was of course full in my uncle's favour, and he was able to bring his ship in. He embraced his terrified friend, cheered and encouraged him, and thinking he could calm his fears by showing his own composure, gave orders that he was to be carried to the bathroom. After his bath he lay down and dined; he was quite cheerful, or at any rate he pretended he was, which was no less courageous.

Meanwhile on Mount Vesuvius broad sheets of fire and leaping flames blazed at several points, their bright glare emphasized by the darkness of night. My uncle tried to allay the fears of his companions by repeatedly declaring that these were nothing but bonfires left by the peasants in their terror, or else empty houses on fire in the districts they had abandoned. Then he went to rest and certainly slept, for as he was a stout man his breathing was rather loud and heavy and could be heard by people coming and going outside his door. By this time the courtyard giving access to his room was full of ashes mixed with pumice-stones, so that its level had risen, and if he had stayed in the room any longer he would never have got out. He was wakened, came out and joined Pomponianus and the rest of the household who had sat up all night. They debated whether to stay indoors or take their chance in the open, for the buildings were now shaking with violent shocks, and seemed to be swaying to and fro as if they were torn from their foundations. Outside on the other hand, there was the danger of falling pumice-stones, even though these were light and porous; however, after comparing the risks they chose the latter. In my uncle's case one reason outweighed the other, but for the others it was a choice of fears. As a protection against falling objects they put pillows on their heads tied down with cloths.

Elsewhere there was daylight by this time, but they were still in darkness, blacker and denser than any night that ever was, which they relieved by lighting torches and various kinds of lamp. My uncle decided to go down to the shore and investigate on the spot the possibility of any escape by sea, but he found the waves still wild and dangerous. A sheet was spread on the ground for him to lie down, and he repeatedly asked for cold water to drink. Then the flames and smell of sulphur which gave warning of the approaching fire drove the others to take flight and roused him to stand up. He stood leaning on two slaves and then suddenly collapsed, I imagine because the dense fumes choked his breathing by blocking his windpipe which was constitutionally weak and narrow and often inflamed. When daylight returned on the 26th—two days after the last day he had seen—his body was found intact and uninjured, still fully clothed and looking more like sleep than death.

Meanwhile my mother and I were at Misenum, but this is not of any historic interest, and you only wanted to hear about my uncle's death. I will say no more, except to add that I have described in detail every incident which I either witnessed myself or heard about immediately after the event, when reports were most likely to be accurate. It is for you to select what best suits your purpose, for there is a great difference between a letter to a friend and history written for all to read.[2]

Book VI.20 To Cornelius Tacitus

So the letter which you asked me to write on my uncle's death has made you eager to hear about the terrors and also the hazards I had to face when left at Misenum, for I broke off at the beginning of this part of my story . . .

After my uncle's departure I spent the rest of the day with my books, as this was my reason for staying behind. Then I took a bath, dined, and then dozed fitfully for a

Detail of "The Eruption of Vesuvius and the Death of Pliny [the Elder]," a painting by Pierre-Henri de Valenciennes, 1813, from Musée des Augustins, Toulouse, France.

while. For several days past there had been earth tremors which were not particularly alarming because they are frequent in Campania: but that night the shocks were so violent that everything felt as if it were not only shaken but overturned. My mother hurried into my room and found me already getting up to wake her if she were still asleep. We sat down in the forecourt of the house, between the buildings and the sea close by. I don't know whether I should call this courage or folly on my part (I was only seventeen at the time) but I called for a volume of Livy and went on reading as if I had nothing else to do. I even went on with the extracts I had been making. Up came a friend of my uncle's who had just come from Spain to join him. When he saw us sitting there and me actually reading, he scolded us both—me for my foolhardiness and my mother for allowing it. Nevertheless, I remained absorbed in my book.

By now it was dawn, but the light was still dim and faint. The buildings round us were already tottering, and the open space we were in was too small for us not to be in real and imminent danger if the house collapsed. This finally decided us to leave the town. We were followed by a panic-stricken mob of people wanting to act on someone else's decision in preference to their own (a point in which fear looks like prudence), who hurried us on our way by pressing hard behind in a dense crowd. Once beyond the buildings we stopped, and there we had some extraordinary experiences which thoroughly alarmed us. The carriages we had ordered to be brought out began to run in different directions though the ground was quite level, and would not remain stationary even when wedged with stones. We also saw the sea sucked away and apparently forced back by the earthquake: at any rate it receded from the shore so that quantitites of sea creatures were left stranded on dry sand. On the landward side a fearful black cloud was rent by forked and quivering bursts of flame, and parted to reveal great tongues of fire, like flashes of lightning magnified in size.

" . . . The fiery torrent rolled on its course to the sea, laying waste and burying towns and villages in its accumulation . . ."

—Campi Phlegraei

"Pliny the Younger and his Mother at Misenum, A.D. 79," an oil painting by Angelica Kauffmann, 1785, from the Art Museum, Princeton University.

At this point my uncle's friend from Spain spoke up still more urgently: "If your brother, if your uncle is still alive, he will want you both to be saved; if he is dead, he would want you to survive him—so why put off your escape?" We replied that we would not think of considering our own safety as long as we were uncertain of his. Without waiting any longer, our friend rushed off and hurried out of danger as fast as he could.

Soon afterwards the cloud sank down to earth and covered the sea; it had already blotted out Capri and hidden the promontory of Misenum from sight. Then my mother implored, entreated, and commanded me to escape as best I could—a young man might escape, whereas she was old and slow and could die in peace as long as she had not been the cause of my death too. I told her I refused to save myself without her, and grasping her hand forced her to quicken her pace. She gave in reluctantly, blaming herself for delaying me. Ashes were already falling, not as yet very thickly. I looked round: a dense black cloud was coming up behind us, spreading over the earth like a flood. "Let us leave the road while we can still see," I said, "or we shall be knocked down and trampled underfoot in the dark by the crowd behind." We had scarcely sat down to rest when darkness fell, not the dark of a moonless or cloudy night, but as if the lamp had been put out in a closed room. You could hear the shrieks of women, the wailing of infants, and the shouting of men; some were calling their parents, others their children or their wives, trying to recognize them by their voices. People bewailed their own fate or that of their relatives, and there were some who prayed for death in their terror of dying. Many besought the aid of the gods, but still more imagined there were no gods left, and that the universe was plunged into eternal darkness for evermore. There were people, too, who added to the real perils by inventing fictitious dangers: some reported that part of Misenum had collapsed or another part was on fire, and though their tales were false they found others to believe them. A gleam of light returned, but we took this to be a warning of the approaching flames rather than daylight. However, the flames remained some distance off; then darkness came on once more and ashes began to fall again, this time in heavy showers. We rose from time to time and shook them off, otherwise we should have been buried and crushed beneath their weight. I could boast that not a groan or cry of fear escaped me in these perils, had I not derived some poor consolation in my mortal lot from the belief that the whole world was dying with me and I with it.

At last the darkness thinned and dispersed into smoke or cloud; then there was genuine daylight, and the sun actually shone out, but yellowish as it is during an eclipse. We were terrified to see everything changed, buried deep in ashes like snowdrifts. We returned to Misenum where we attended to our physical needs as best we could, and then spent an anxious night alternating between hope and fear. Fear predominated, for the earthquakes went on . . . But even then, in spite of the dangers we had been through and were still expecting, my mother and I had still no intention of leaving until we had news of my uncle . . . [3]

" . . . for towns and fields had disappeared under one expanse of white ashes, or were doubtfully marked, like the more prominent objects after an Alpine fall of snow . . . resembling a ploughed field or boisterous sea arrested by a sudden frost."

—Campi Phlegraei

"cuncta jacent flammis et tristi mersa favilla"
(all lies buried in flames and melancholy ashes)
—Martial, *Epigrams* IV.44

Of the 20,000 inhabitants of Pompeii, some 2,000 probably lost their lives, struck down by falling stones, asphyxiated by the noxious fumes, suffocated by drifting ash, or trampled down in the panic of flight. Men, women, children, slaves, dogs and other animals died in the buildings, in the deadly places of refuge, in the streets, on the roads leading out of town away from the fiery mountain, anywhere and nowhere. The buildings and houses did not burn but gradually filled up with the debris of the eruption: first a pumice layer three meters thick in places, then a layer of ashes almost 2.5

23

meters deep, and last over the years a preserving mantle of fertile soil accumulated to the height of 2 meters, lying over bodies and broken structures borne down by the weight of volcanic material and time. The neighboring communities and country estates west and south of Vesuvius were similarly destroyed, but not all in the same way. Herculaneum was buried by a flood of superheated mud—mud lava—which dried into rock-like hardness, preserving the town as if it were frozen deep beneath the surface, and eventually most difficult to excavate.

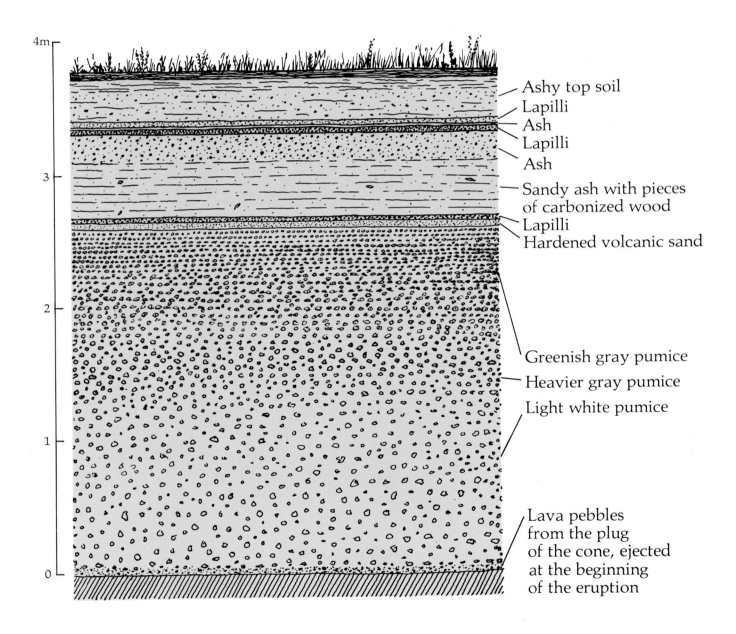

4m

Ashy top soil
Lapilli
Ash
Lapilli
Ash

3

Sandy ash with pieces
of carbonized wood
Lapilli
Hardened volcanic sand

2

Greenish gray pumice
Heavier gray pumice
Light white pumice

1

Lava pebbles
from the plug
of the cone, ejected
at the beginning
of the eruption

0

Roman Pompeii disappeared from view but not before survivors and looters had burrowed into the cooled wreckage of the town, seeking favorite possessions or valuables. Soon, however, perhaps even before Pliny published his letters to Tacitus early in the second century, the destruction of Pompeii had come to be interpreted as more than a natural event, rather as an instance of divine punishment. In the Sibylline Oracles, the eruption and resulting obliteration of Pompeii were viewed not as punishment for the sins of the Pompeians but for the impiety of Titus who had conquered and sacked Jerusalem in A.D. 70 and had become emperor in 79 (*Oracula Sibyllina* IV). What had been taken to be evidence of divine retribution in the Oracle by the third century came to be considered a frightful instance of the manifestation of the demonic forces in nature. So then the Roman historian, Cassius Dio:

Book LXVI.21.1

In Campania remarkable and frightful occurrences took place; for a great fire suddenly flared up at the very end of the summer. It happened on this wise. Mt. Vesuvius stands over against Neapolis near the sea and it has inexhaustible fountains of fire . . .

LXVI.22.2-4

This is what befell. Numbers of huge men quite surpassing any human stature—such creatures, in fact, as the Giants are pictured to have been—appeared, now on the mountain, now in the surrounding country, and again in the cities, wandering over the earth day and night and also flitting through the air. There were frequent rumblings, some of them subterranean, that resembled thunder, and some on the surface, that sounded like bellowings; the sea also joined in the roar and the sky re-echoed it. Then suddenly a portentous crash was heard, as if the mountain were tumbling in ruins; at first huge stones were hurled aloft, rising as high as the very summits, then came a great quantity of fire and endless smoke, so that the whole atmosphere was obscured and the sun was entirely hidden, as if eclipsed.

LXVI.23.1-5

Thus day was turned into night and light into darkness. Some thought that the Giants were rising again in revolt . . . while others believed that the whole universe was being resolved into chaos or fire. Therefore they fled, some from the houses into the streets,

others from outside into the houses, now from the sea to the land and now from the land to the sea; for in their excitement they regarded any place where they were not as safer than where they were. While this was going on, an inconceivable quantity of ashes was blown out, which covered both sea and land and filled all the air. It wrought much injury of various kinds as chance befell, to men and farms and cattle, and in particular it destroyed all fish and birds. Furthermore, it buried two entire cities, Herculaneum and Pompeii, the latter place while its populace was seated in the theater. Indeed, the amount of dust, taken all together, was so great that some of it reached Africa and Syria and Egypt, and it also reached Rome, filling the air overhead and darkening the sun. There, too, no little fear was occasioned, that lasted for several days, since the people did not know and could not imagine what had happened, but, like those close at hand, believed that the whole world was being turned upside down, that the sun was disappearing into the earth and that the earth was being lifted to the sky . . . [4]

Soon the name of Pompeii itself was forgotten, but not that once at the foot of Mount Vesuvius beside the Sarno there had been an ancient town, a *civitas* or *civitá* in Italian. As *Civitá* or *Cittade*, its memory survived into the Renaissance, to be resurrected by Jacopo Sannazzaro in his great pastoral work, *Arcadia* X.16–39 (circa 1482), XI (circa 1502/4), as a place of ancient settlement, now ruined and covered with greenery, where only the sound of the Faun may be heard playing in the thickets. Stimulated by the *Arcadia*, by the texts of Pliny's letters, and perhaps by local legends, references to both Pompeii and Herculaneum began to appear in sixteenth-century Italian maps of the region. In 1592 or 1594 Count Muzio Tuttavilla tried to divert the course of the Sarno River and in the process workmen turned up bits and pieces of ruined buildings, including fragments of wall-paintings and other debris. These discoveries were brought

"The Last Days of Pompeii," an oil painting by James Hamilton, 1864, from the Brooklyn Museum.

Fausto Niccolini re-created the continuing volcanic activity of Vesuvius during the nineteenth century in this 1862 painting of visitors viewing the Forum ruins.

to the attention of the architect Domenico Fontana, but nothing came of it since no connection was made between Città and buried Pompeii, although the channel-digging operations passed very close to the Temple of Isis and to the Amphitheater. A few years later an inscription was found containing the words *decurio Pompeis* but it was thought to belong to a "Villa of Pompeius;" that mistaken attribution, because of the importance of Pompey in Roman history, occupied the minds of the ancient historians and topographers of Campania throughout the seventeenth century.

In 1631 Vesuvius erupted again with devastating effect, causing greater casualties than 79 and spewing out quantitites of lava in a westerly direction, by-passing Città/ Pompeii but covering Resina beside the site of buried Herculaneum. Indeed, Vesuvius

Portrait of Domenico Fontana, famed Roman architect who scratched the surface of Pompeii in constructing a conduit for Count Tuttavilla—an engraving from "Uomini Illustrati" by Ginori, 1763.

An engraving of Charles III, absolute monarch of the Kingdom of the Two Sicilies from 1735 to 1759 when he ascended to the Spanish Throne, prime mover in the uncovering of Herculaneum and the early excavations in Pompeii.

has erupted more than seventy times since 79, most damagingly in 203, 512, 1631, 1707, 1794, 1855, 1872, 1906, and 1944. These catastrophes reminded men of the destruction of Pompeii, while the power of nature, manifest in volcanic activity, overwhelmed their imaginations. If the latter sensation was particularly dear to the artists and writers of the Romantic period, it did little to advance the recovery of the ancient sites, at least until the eighteenth century. Ironically, the eruption of 1944 during the terrible year of the Italian campaign did no damage to Pompeii; that was done by the 162 bombs, dropped by Allied planes in August and September of 1943 in an effort to cut the railroad but which fell on Pompeii instead. The exposed Houses of the Faun and of the Moralist as well as the Museum were struck, ancient treasures, once saved from the earth, again open to destruction from the air.

But destruction of the ancient Campanian sites by the hands of men had begun much earlier. In 1709 the Austrian Prince d'Elbeuf ordered a well to be sunk on his property in Resina, lying on top of Herculaneum, and his workmen encountered the stage wall of the ancient theater, then, as now, perhaps the best preserved of all Roman theaters. During the next seven years the Prince mined the theater of Herculaneum, removing the marble decorations of the stage and many large statues. Many of these statues were sent north as gifts to his patron in Vienna, Prinz Eugen von Savoyen, among them the famous Herculaneum maidens acquired in 1736 for the royal Antikensammlung in Dresden. D'Elbeuf's rapacious enterprise was soon stopped, and under the Spanish-Bourbon king of the Two Sicilies, Charles III, excavations of Herculaneum were officially begun on October 1, 1738, directed by the Spanish engineer, Rocco Gioacchino de Alcubierre, assisted by the Swiss architect Karl Weber and, later, by Francesco La Vega. But these were not excavations in the modern sense which remove layers of soil to uncover the past. Rather, they were tunneling operations which opened up underground galleries, connected by narrow shafts and lateral passages, that gave only partial access to the ancient buildings buried in the hardened flow of mud lava, more than fifty feet thick in places.

Thus, the ruins of Herculaneum were mined for the hidden treasures of ancient art they contained; sculptures and precious objects were removed, panel paintings cut from the walls of which they once formed an integral part, while the sense of the whole in the form of plans or elevations or partial reconstructions was very difficult to obtain. Although a general plan of Herculaneum was eventually drawn by La Vega, and Karl Weber made a useful plan of the Villa of the Papyri—explored and looted of its marble

An impression of the subterranean Herculaneum Theater by torchlight, an illustration from La Destruccion de Pompeya, *a novel by Miceto de Zamarcois published in Mexico in 1871.*

The larger-than-life equestrian statue of Marcus Nonius Balbus, discovered in the excavations at Herculaneum in 1739, aroused great excitement and was followed in due course by the finding of a similar statue of his son. Though both were immediately whisked off to Portici, they stirred interest throughout Europe when Marcello Venuti published their likenesses in 1748.

and bronze sculptures, of its papyrus scrolls, from 1750–1765—knowledge of Herculaneum itself was very limited. The repossession of its art became paramount, and the booty from the explorations was collected in a specially established Royal Museum at Portici, just to the north of Herculaneum. This first period of exploration at Herculaneum ceased in 1765 without developing a true "archaeology." The shafts and galleries were filled up with earth, and the site was left almost as it had been, but not quite. There were, after all, those beautiful works of ancient art!

Charles de Brosses wrote his *Lettres familières écrites d'Italie* from Naples in 1739 and 1740. Among them the letter to Bouhier, dated November 28, 1739, describes his visit to the subterranean town of Herculaneum, reached through tunnels like a mine, and the paintings to be seen there. Even more important is his presentation before the Académie des Inscriptions et Belles-lettres in Paris, probably read on November 20, 1749, which brought to the attention of the savants of Europe more complete knowledge of Herculaneum and of the first scholarly work on the excavations, the *Descrizione delle prime scoperte dell'Antica città d'Ercolano*, published by Marcello Venuti in 1748. By 1755 the

Veduta delle due facce laterali dell'insigne maravigliosa Statua Eguestre, cavata da un intero marmo, grande presso che al naturale, trovata l'anno 1739, negli Scavi fatti presso la Real Villa di Portici d' ordine del Re delle due Sicilie, collocata nel Loggiato di essa, dedicata dagli Ercolanesi a M. Nonio Balbo Pretore, e Proconsolo.

Herculaneum Academy (Accademia Ercolanese) had been founded under royal auspices, and a year later, Johann Joachim Winckelmann, the premier expert in classical art of all Europe, visited Herculaneum and the museum in Portici. Beginning in 1757 the Academy undertook the publication of the lavishly illustrated folio volumes, the *Antichità di Ercolano*, 8 volumes, Naples, 1757–1792, which brought the treasures of the ancient town to the world, and the world eventually to Campania.

On March 23, 1748, Alcubierre and Giacopo Martorelli of Naples began excavating Cività, possibly in the belief that Stabiae lay underneath. They dug near the Temple of Fortuna and beside the intersection of the Via Stabiana and the Via di Nola, close to the center of ancient Pompeii. The techniques and objectives were those established for Herculaneum, buried beneath hardened mud lava, not suitable for the large middle-class market town, Pompeii, resting under layers of soft pumice, ash, and earth.

On August 20, 1763, the excavators of Cività found an inscription of Suedius Clemens on the Street of the Tombs near the Herculaneum Gate. This inscription included the words, RES PUBLICA POMPEIANORUM, and thus fixed the identification of Cività as Pompeii. From this time forth, the site was returned to history. From this time forth the excavated areas of Pompeii were left uncovered and the "pleasure of ruins" provided a civilizing entrance into the stupendous past.

Stemmed goblet in cobalt blue glass, from one of the sites in the Vesuvius area. Two horizontal wheel-cut lines decorate the outside of the body which was blown into a mold. The stem is formed from two large beads of glass with the foot added separately. This drinking cup was intended for table use.

The Excursion

Canto I

Companion of the muse, creative power
Imagination! at whose great command
Arise unnumber'd images of things,
Thy hourly offspring: . . .

In these blest plains, a spacious city spreads
Its round extent magnificent, and seems
The seat of empire. Dazzling in the sky,
With far-seen blaze her towery structures shine,
Elaborate works of art! each opening gate
Sends forth its thousands: peace and plenty round
Environ her. In each frequented school
Learning exalts his head: and Commerce pours
Into her arms a thousand foreign realms.
How fair and fortunate! how worthy all
of lasting bliss secure! Yet all must fail,
O'erturn'd and lost—nor shall their place be
    found!

A sullen calm unusual, dark and dead,
Arises inauspicious o'er the heavens . . .
And now, within the bosom of the globe,
Where sulphur stor'd and nitre peaceful slept,
For ages, in their subterranean bed,
Ferments th'approaching tempest. Vapory steams,
Inflammable, perhaps by winds sublim'd,
Their deadly breath apply. Th'enkindled mass,
Mine fir'd by mine in train, with boundless rage,
With horror unconceiv'd, disploded bursts
Its central prison—Shook from shore to shore,
Reels the broad continent with all its load,
Hill, forests, cities. The lone desert quakes:
Her savage sons howl to the thunder's groan,
And lightning's ruddy glare: while from beneath,
Deaf distant roarings, through the void profound,
Rueful are heard, as when Despair complains.

Gather'd in the air, o'er that proud Capital,
Frowns an involving cloud of gloomy depth,
Casting dun night and terror o'er the heads
Of her inhabitants. Aghast they stand,
Sad-gazing on the mournful skies around;
A moment's dreadful silence! Then loud screams,
And eager supplications rend the skies.
Lo, crowds on crowds, in hurry'd stream along,
From street to street, from gate to gate roll'd on,
This, that way burst in waves, by horror wing'd
To distant hill or cave: while half the globe,
Her frame convulsive rocking to and fro,
Trembles with second agony. Upheav'd
In surges, her vext furnace rolls a sea.
Ruin ensues; towers, temples, palaces,
Flung from their deep foundations, roof on roof
Crush'd horrible, and pile on pile o'erturned,
Fall total—In that universal groan,
Sounding to heaven, expir'd a thousand lives,
O'erwhelmed at once, one undistinguish'd wreck!

. . . A shuddering band! Distraction in each eye
Stares wildly motionless; they pant, they catch
A gulp of air, and gasp with dying aim
The wreck that drives along, to gain from fate
Short interval! a moment's doubtful life.
For now, earth's solid sphere asunder rent
With final dissolution, the huge mass
Fails undermin'd—down her buildings sink!
Sinks the full pride her ample walls enclos'd,
In one wild havoc crash'd, with burst beyond
Heaven's loudest thunder! Uproar unconceiv'd!
Image of nature's general frame destroy'd!
How greatly terrible, how dark and deep
The purposes of heaven![1]

Discovery:
Treasure Hunting and Neoclassicism, 1748–1820

MALLET'S extravagant poem, a proto-romantic exercise in horrified delight, anticipated many of the themes of response and interpretation that inspired the literary figures of western Europe, once they had become aware of the rediscovery of Herculaneum and Pompeii. A lively civilization, vital inhabitants, vivid surroundings—all that one might hope for in the human condition—yet situated at the edge of hazard, the life of Pompeii was snuffed out by the catastrophic eruption, by the unheeding forces of nature, and by implacable fate. This rapid transition from life to death, from construction to destruction, from activity to desolation, caught the minds and hearts of cultured authors and artists. They felt themselves once more to be in touch with the Classical past in terms of its perennial physical presence, giving substance to their image of that past, hitherto transmitted by the literary tradition. But contemplation of that past as a ruin carried with it an implication of the transiency of all things as a source of fear and wonder, perhaps most fully articulated in the famous work of the Comte de Volney, *Les Ruines: ou Méditations sur les Révolutions des Empire* (1792).

Beyond the moralizing contemplation of the ruins of Pompeii with its emphasis upon the destruction of the ancient town, a keen delight in its resurrection gave pleasure to many. For them Antiquity had become so very real, and the successive states of Pompeii's prior existence, destruction, concealment, and reappearance could be grasped as acts in a cosmic melodrama, addressing history and the imagination at one and the same moment. Thus, in the nearly seventy years from the beginnings of the excavations of Pompeii to the end of the Napoleonic era, imagination—fed by luxurious publications, scholarly dispute, the acquisition and collection of art treatures, and the formal visit to the ancient sites—was paramount over historical investigation. And a peculiar mixture of the literary tradition on Pompeii's destruction together with the finds emerging from Herculaneum had precedence.

Marcello Venuti's original scholarly treatment of the finds at Herculaneum, first published in Italian in 1748, then presented to the French Academy of Inscriptions by de Brosses in 1749, was translated into English by Wickes Skurray in 1750, indicating the widespread interest in the discoveries. Venuti refers to that interest in the preface to his volume where he justified his publication on the grounds that, "Since the finding of antiquities is one of learned men's noblest pleasures, what glory there must be for the King of the Two Sicilies to find, not simply fragments, but an entire city." The book goes on to describe the history of Herculaneum and the discovery of its antiquities, emphasizing the importance of the epigraphical evidence and the theater, and remarking on the freshness of the paintings, their color and subject matter, but not their art. Although Venuti wished to inform the world of the discoveries made under the patronage of his royal master, Charles III, his successors jealously held on to Herculaneum as a private concession and exercised the closest proprietorship over the finds. This task was made easy by the difficulty of access to Herculaneum itself through the closely guarded and

*Detail of "The Finding of Telephus," a fresco curved to fit a niche in the
Herculaneum Basilica, found in the 1730's. According to legend, Telephus
was one of Hercules' many illegitimate sons; his mother was Auge, a virgin
priestess of Athene, who was sent away when her father became aware of her
pregnancy. She bore Telephus while traveling and abandoned him in a
thicket in the wilds of Arcadia on a mountaintop. Only through
nourishment supplied by a doe, shown here lovingly licking his knee, did
Telephus manage to survive.*

dangerous tunnels and to the royal museum at Portici, where no one was permitted to draw or copy any of the works of art on display. The way was made for the establishment of the Accademia Ercolanese in 1755 and for their supervision of the magnificently illustrated volumes of the *Antichità di Ercolano* which became the medium for the reinforcement of the memories of those visitors fortunate enough to have been to Herculaneum and Portici and for the broadest dissemination of the finds. These volumes were arranged by medium: *Le pitture antiche d'Ercolano e contorni*, 5 volumes, 1757–1779; *De' bronzi di Ercolano e contorni*, 2 volumes, 1767–1771; and *Le lucerne ed i candelabri d'Ercolano e contorni*, 1792. Nothing comparable was issued for Pompeii in the eighteenth century, although for most of the period from 1748 to 1800 active excavations were being conducted.

In addition, objects found at other Campanian sites, including Stabiae and Pompeii, and contained in the museum at Portici, fell under the general heading "antiquities of Herculaneum and its environs." An example of the fallacious provenance given to objects is the association of two famous bronze tripods with Herculaneum, although they were in fact discovered at the Temple of Isis and in the Villa of Julia Felix at Pompeii, themselves major sites in the early excavations of Pompeii, and well-known. Further confounding this problem and adding to the burden of misinformation, O. A. Bayardi's *Catalogo degli antiche monumenti dissotterati della discoperta città di Ercolano* (Naples, 1775), despite its title, does not give the provenance of the finds, described as objects out of context.

Charles III had declared to the famous Florentine Etruscologist, A. F. Gori—who saw the Etruscans everywhere, including in Campania—that "he did not wish Florence to be informed of what he wished to conceal," since the king wanted to be the source of all knowledge of the ancient sites. Thus, Charles III and the Bourbons kept the volumes of the *Antichità di Ercolano* out of the commercial market and gave them away as royal presents and tokens of favor. Indeed, his hostility to outsiders and his desire to control publication are mentioned in a pirated edition, published in English under the title, *The Antiquities of Herculaneum* (London, 1773), by Thomas Martyn and John Lettice. Furthermore, Gori himself in 1752 managed to publish his

40

The object and intent involved in this wall painting from Herculaneum are implicit in the complacent expressions on the faces of the couple. With her feminine attributes clearly visible beneath her see-through attire and her wayward curls held in check by a net, the lady's hand is outstretched to receive a casket (payment in advance?) while her muscular companion prepares to down a drink from his drinking horn (rhyton) with replenishments readily available on the table in the foreground.

Admiranda Antiquitatum Herculanensium with reference to the theater, buildings, statues, pictures, and inscriptions. In the Italian edition of the same book (1748) Gori mentions the letters of famous literati who had visited the excavations, and such letters, once published, became a source of knowledge about the excavations and an arena for the exercise of aesthetic judgment and criticism about the management of the excavations by the king in Naples and his excavators and curators.

Charles de Brosses' letter to President Bouhier, dated November 28, 1739, is essentially a long memoir on the subterranean city of Herculaneum. In it he reviewed briefly the history of the place but concentrated on the paintings—especially the *Education of Achilles by the Centaur Chiron* and *Theseus and the Minotaur*—which he compared with the familiar Roman painting in the Vatican, the *Aldobrandini Wedding*, and most favorably with the classical grace and color of Raphael and Ludovico Carracci rather than with Poussin. De Brosses approved of the excavations and made the most positive aesthetic judgment about the ancient paintings themselves. Not so his countryman, the engraver C. N. Cochin, who traveled to Naples in 1750 with the architect Soufflot and the Marquis de Marigny, brother of Madame de Pompadour; this group was under the influence of the erudite classicist, the Comte de Caylus, who had himself visited Herculaneum in 1715 without entering the excavation tunnels, and was turning against the current taste for the rococo, still dominant in France. Cochin published an account of this

The legendary tale of how Theseus slew the Minotaur has all the ingredients of a contemporary thriller. Supplied with a magic ball of thread by Ariadne, daughter of King Minos who had fallen in love with him at first sight, Theseus followed the ball as it rolled along into the depths of the labyrinth where the Minotaur's lair was located, killed the dreaded beast (with a sword also provided by Ariadne), and found his way back out again by rewinding the thread on his return route. The only repayment Ariadne had requested for her help was that Theseus take her with him when he left the island to go back to Athens—which he did. However, he later abandoned her on the island of Naxos—behavior most unbecoming to any true hero. This wall painting from the exedra off the peristyle in the House of Gavius Rufus shows Theseus in his moment of glory surrounded by grateful Athenians, the Minotaur's intended victims who each year had been sent as tribute to Crete's bull-headed monster. An even more stirring version of this same scene was found in the early excavations at Herculaneum.

43

journey, *Voyage d'Italie*, in 1758 wherein he expressed a very negative opinion about the quality of the paintings and of the architecture which he had seen at Herculaneum. These sentiments had already been expressed in an earlier book, published with the architect J. C. Bellicard in 1753 and issued in an English edition in 1756. Bellicard complains about the inaccuracy of his plans because he was not permitted to measure the buildings, criticizes the composition and design of the wall-paintings as well as their color, disapproves of the non-Grecian elements in the architectural paintings, but rescues his positive view of antiquity by suggesting that the artists at work in Campania were not very good. The conflict between concept and reality so important to the reception of the discoveries at Herculaneum and Pompeii had thus begun.

Jean-Jacques Barthélemy, author of *Voyage du jeune Anacharsis en Grèce* (1788)—the first novel to use the results of the Campanian excavations to establish a more accurate historical setting—also traveled in Italy in 1755–1756, visiting Herculaneum, Portici, and Pompeii. He reported on his site visits in a series of letters, some of them addressed to the Comte de Caylus, best known in a translated English edition, published by Ant. Serrieys in London, 1802, under the title, *Travels in Italy, by the late Abbé Barthélemy, author of Travels of Anacharsis the Younger; in a Series of Letters written to the Celebrated Count Caylus* . . . In Letter V, written at Rome, November 5, 1755, Barthélemy wrote:

There is a magazine of pictures, discovered in ancient Pompii (sic) which was destroyed about the same time with Herculaneum. These paintings are far superior to those of Herculaneum; being well coloured, well drawn, and well ornamented: the greater part are covered with a plaster that can easily be taken off. Mr. de la Condamine procured a fine piece from them just before my arrival, and has had others copied; he has promised to get me some, so that I hope to be able to provide for the academy and you . . .

His Letter VI, from Rome, November 11, 1755, relates that he purchased one of these Pompeian paintings from la Condamine and "it was covered with plaster, which has been taken off: a stripe of it is, however, left on the edges, to satisfy the curiosity of those who wish to see how such things come out of the earth . . . " In his Letter XV, written at Rome, February 10, 1756, Barthélemy acknowledges that the painting was a fake, that he was duped by the Roman antiquaries, and that numerous other men of letters had purchased similar paintings.

Excavation work at Herculaneum, an engraving from Cochin and Bellicard's Observations sur les Antiquités d'Ercolanum, *1753.*

great French encyclopedist, Diderot, who specifically criticized the book of one Fougeroux de Bordaroy, *Recherches sur les ruines d'Herculanum*, in Grimm's *Correspondance Littéraire* of 1769 because it was a dry catalogue of objects, despite the great importance given to the same class of utilitarian objects of his own time in the *Encyclopédie*. Not only did the *Encyclopédie* ignore the finds from Herculaneum and Pompeii, but Diderot excluded *les antiquités*—pots and pans, etc.—from the realm of l'antiquité, the classical tradition preserved through ancient literature, which for him truly and alone represented the classical past. That mistakenly elitist attitude still survives among those who denigrate the value of modern archaeology as a major branch of Classical studies.

Yet there was a growing interest in the discoveries which stimulated more publication, often in the context of general works on Italy as a whole, stimulated in part by a broadening range of historical topics and by the increased frequency of the tourist.

The bronze cooking utensils pictured here were found in the House of the Vettii and were placed back on the hearth just as they would have been positioned when in use—one pot on an iron tripod, others being kept warm, with charcoal ready to be fired beneath.

Two large works are symptomatic of this development: Abbé Richard's *Description Historique et Critique de l'Italie ou Nouveaux Memoires sur l'Etat actuel de son Gouvernement, des Sciences, des Arts, du Commerce, de la Population et de l'Histoire Naturelle*, 6 volumes, Paris, 1769, which reaches Naples, Vesuvius, Herculaneum, and Portici late in Volume IV, and there essentially provides a preparatory guide for the non-specialist visitor. Much the same can be said of D. J. J. Volkmann's *Historische-kritische Nachrichten von Italien welche eine Beschreibung dieses Landes der Sitten, Regierungsform, Handlung, des Zustandes der Wissenschaften und insonderheit der Werke der Kunst*, Volume III, Leipzig, 1778, which covers the same ground. But Volkmann has more to say about Pompeii and places great emphasis on the works of art, incorporating much of the extant scholarly literature, including the opinions of Cochin and of Winckelmann. Such books were intended for an educated audience, drawn to Italy and eager to be informed about the country, its history, and its art before, during, and after a tour of the famous sites. Increasingly among these famous sites were Herculaneum and Pompeii, progressively more accessible after 1775. The position of these ancient towns on the "Grand Tour" contributed to their greater role in the culture of the time and to their continued exploitation. The guidebook and the guide followed suit as the resource of the traveler who, as tourist, came to see for himself.

So Horace Walpole in 1740 wrote to Benjamin West,

Have you heard of a subterranean town? A whole Roman town, with all its edifices, remaining under ground? . . . You remember in Titus' time there were several cities destroyed by an eruption of Vesuvius attended with an earthquake. Well, this was one of them, not very considerable, and then called Herculaneum. Above it has since been built Portici, about three miles from Naples, where the king has a villa. This underground city is perhaps one of the noblest curiosities that ever has been discovered . . . There is one inside of a temple quite perfect . . . It is built of brick plastered over and painted with architecture: almost all the insides of the houses are in the same manner; and, what is very particular, the general ground of all the painting is red . . . They have found among other things some fine statues, some human bones, some rice, medals, and a few paintings extremely fine . . . There is nothing of the kind known in the world; I mean a Roman city entire of that age, and that has not been corrupted with modern repairs . . . 'Tis certainly an advantage to the learned world that this has been laid up so long.

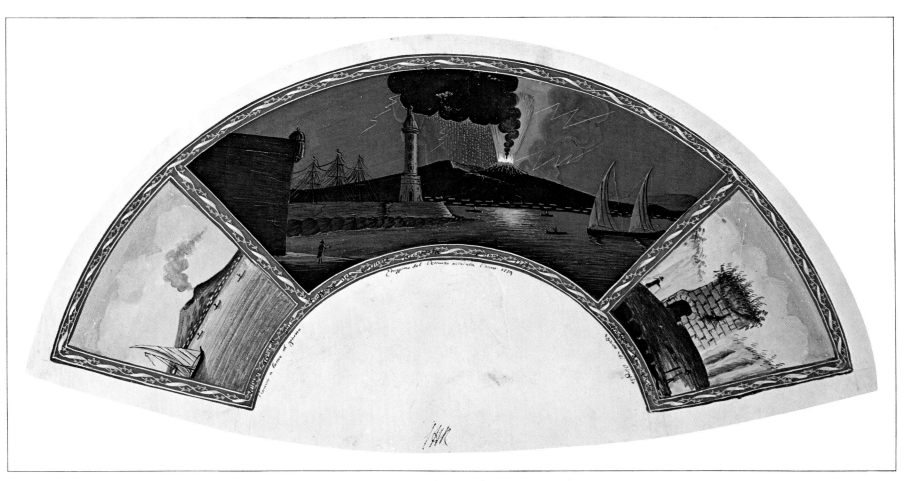

*A trio of Grand Tour attractions are illustrated on this 18th-century Italian
fan leaf: the Bay of Naples, a vista of Vesuvius, and the tomb of Virgil—
Gouache drawing on parchment, from The Metropolitan Museum of Art.*

In the same year 1740, John Dyer wrote his extravagant poem, "The Ruins of
Rome," possibly stimulated by reports of the excavations and the contrast they posed
between the pristine original condition of the ancient towns and their present state.
Similar preoccupations inspired Edward Gibbon, musing amidst the ruins of the Capitol
at Rome on the evening of October 15, 1764, to conceive of writing *The Decline and Fall*.
Gibbon was there because he had come to Italy on "the grand tour," and although he did
not go to Campania, his countryman, Robert Adam, visited Herculaneum in 1755 and
Vesuvius, and possibly even Pompeii, although later references to Pompeian forms in his
architecture depended more on subsequent publications than on first-hand experience.

Typical of the mixed feelings developed by the gentleman-tourist's visit to Pompeii is the opening of William Beckford's "letter" from Naples, November 9, 1780:

We made our excursion to Pompeii, passing through Portici, and over the last lava of Mount Vesuvius. I experienced a strange mixture of sensations, on surveying at once, the mischiefs of the late eruption, in the ruin of villages, farms, and vineyards; and, all around them, the most luxuriant and delightful scenery of nature. It was impossible to resist the impressions of melancholy from viewing the former, or not to admit that gaiety of spirits which was inspired by the sight of the latter . . .

Goethe, beginning his reach toward greatness, toured Pompeii with his artist-companion, Johann Heinrich Wilhelm Tischbein, on March 11 and 13, 1787. Prepared for his visit by a deep knowledge of Winckelmann's writings, guided by Volkmann's *Historische-kritische Nachrichten von Italien* (1770–71), sensitized visually by plates and drawings of the site, Goethe described his experience in his *Italienische Reise* (1816–17). He saw the grave of the priestess Mamia near the Herculaneum Gate, the Temple of Isis, the Villa of Diomedes, enjoyed the painted rooms with their empaneled subjects, and approved of the straight, paved streets, but he thought the windowless houses rather dark and both private and public buildings much too small. Philipp Hackert's watercolors, many of them preserved in the Goethe-Nationalmuseum at Weimar, represented the current state of the excavations, a topic that appealed to many foreign artists drawn to Campania in the late eighteenth century, to Pompeii and to Vesuvius. These artists found the ancient sites most picturesque and variously fascinating, valuable for the development of their art and for ready sale to tourists. But the Pompeian experience was indelibly fixed in Goethe's mind for all his life, although he never returned. However, the poet was deeply moved by the fact of survival ("Der Ort inspiriert Nachlässigkeit"), by the prospect of Pompeii both destroyed and mummified by the sudden eruption, and by the poignant contrast between the deadly ashes and the blue Campanian sky. This elegeic tone pervades Schiller's "Pompeji und Herkulanum" (1796) and even touches the ebullient Chateaubriand who visited Herculaneum, Portici, and Pompeii on January 11, 1804, and wondered at the "Musée de la terre" which preserved a Roman town entire. This attitude is effectively summed up by the Rev. John C. Eustace in his *A Classical Tour through Italy An. MDCCCII* which went into several editions:

58

"But independent even of this advantage (objects preserved in their original context, rather than arranged in a museum) and stripped as it is of almost all its movable ornaments, Pompeii possesses a secret power that captivates, I had almost said, melts the soul. In other times and in other places, one single edifice, a temple, a theater, a tomb, that had escaped the wreck of ages, would have enchanted us; . . . but to discover a single ancient house, the abode of a Roman in his privacy, the scene of his domestic hours, was an object of fond, but hopeless longing. Here, not a temple, nor a theater, nor a column, nor a house, but a whole city rises before us, untouched, unaltered . . . We range through the same streets, tread the very same pavement, behold the same walls, enter the same doors, and repose in the same apartments . . . you may, without any great effort of imagination, expect to meet some of the former inhabitants, or perhaps the master of the house himself, and almost feel like intruders . . . All around is silence, not the silence of solitude and repose, but of death and devastation: the silence of a great city without one single inhabitant." [2]

In 1807 Madame de Staël peopled those empty streets in her partly autobiographical novel, *Corinne ou l'Italie*, invoking her own experience as a tourist at Pompeii in 1804–05.

In the 1780's cultivated tourists like Beckford and Goethe, who came to visit Naples and see the ancient monuments of Campania, inevitably fell into the circle of Sir William Hamilton, the English consul in Naples from 1764 to 1800. Hamilton was an avid collector of classical antiquities and of a beautiful woman, Emma Hart, who became (with permission) the mistress of Admiral Lord Nelson and famous for her classical "attitudes," posed portraits of the figures on her husband's beloved vases. Hamilton was a great collector of vases, still commonly called "Etruscan" but more and more recognized to be Greek, as defined by Winckelmann and others. His First Collection, consisting of more than 730 painted vases, 627 bronzes, 150 ivories, 150 gems, 300 pieces of glass, 175 terra cottas, more than 6,000 coins, miscellaneous jewelry, and some marbles—all acquired in Italy—was sold to the British Museum shortly after his return to England in 1772. This collection formed the basis of the Department of Antiquities at the Museum and became widely known through its English and French language publication by Hamilton and Pierre François Hughes d'Hancarville, *Collection of Etruscan, Grecian and Roman Antiquities in the Cabinet of the Honorable William Hamilton at Naples*, 4 volumes, Naples, 1766–67. This sumptuous publication stimulated Josiah Wedgwood's manufacture of "Greek," "Etruscan," and "Pompeian" vases. Because of

For over thirty years while serving as British Minister Plenipotentiary to the Kingdom of the Two Sicilies, Sir William Hamilton was a dedicated volcano-watcher, observing, recording and even occasionally risking his life in order to supply information relating to the phenomena of volcanic eruptions. He is seen here on the floor of the crater acting in an instructive capacity (by Pietro Fabris from Campi Phlegraei).

Illuminated by the fiery eruptions, Sir William Hamilton indicates the current of lava running down to Resina (built atop previously mud-buried Herculaneum) to the king and queen on the evening of May 11, 1771 (by Pietro Fabris from Campi Phlegraei).

Lord Hamilton's second wife, the legendary Lady Emma, entered whole-heartedly into her husband's activities and soon became a dig-and-volcano devotee as well. She is observing the excavation work at Paestum in this 1790's engraving.

the splendor of the folio plates, accompanied by d'Hancarville's Winckelmannic text, it soon served as a fountainhead of English and continental Neoclassicism.

Returning to Naples, Hamilton formed his Second Collection of vases and other antiquities, while he continued to maintain his house as an intellectual and social center of classical studies for the foreigner touring in Campania. He also employed Tischbein, Goethe's former companion, to decorate a room in his town house and, later, to engrave the plates in the catalogue of the Second Collection, issued under the title, *Collection of Engravings from Ancient Vases mostly of Pure Greek Workmanship discovered in Sepulchres in the Kingdom of the Two Sicilies, now in Possession of Sir William Hamilton*, 4 volumes, Naples, 1791–1795; the German edition appeared in three volumes from 1797 to 1800. Although the Second Collection had been gathered in two short years, 1789 and 1790, it was larger and probably more important than the First, indicating the great opportunities available to a collector of antiquities in the treasure-house of Italy. The Second Collection, however, was widely dispersed into private hands and a large part of it was shipped to England and went down at sea in the *Colossus*. That sunken ship has recently been discovered, and divers are bringing up many of the vases of Hamilton's Second Collection, known from Tischbein's engravings and now under restoration in the British Museum.

In 1777 William Hamilton joined the Society of Dilettanti, founded in London about 1734 as a social club but by the 1760's a major center for the promotion of classical archaeology in the hellenic world of Greece, Asia Minor, and the Levant. In 1748, that magic year for Pompeii, James Stuart, painter, and Nicholas Revett, architect, together

62

Josiah Wedgwood was among the first to jump on the classical bandwagon. Naming his new factory "Etruria," he borrowed Sir William Hamilton's far-famed Portland Vase for twelve months in order to make jasperware replicas. Jasperware, a white, mat, unglazed pottery material resembling unglazed porcelain, could be stained in varying tints, with white ornamentation made in separate molds applied to the body of the piece to produce antique designs in relief. The Wedgwood "Etrurian" urn with cover and pedestal in green, white and cane color jasperware pictured is on display at The Metropolitan Museum of Art.

with Gavin Hamilton, painter and art dealer, came to Naples to arrange for the study and publication of the Antiquities of Athens with the support of the English dilettanti. Stuart and Revett's *Antiquities of Athens*, volume I, appeared in 1762 (London)—volume II in 1787, III in 1794, IV in 1816—and had an enormous impact. Although Stuart and Revett were in Naples, there is no evidence that they ever visited Herculaneum or Pompeii. Furthermore, they were active partisans in a quarrel which they and others developed between the "Greeks" and the "Romans." Stuart expressed his point of view most explicitly in the preface to volume I of the *Antiquities*:

Greece was the great Mistress of the Arts, and Rome, in this respect, no more than her disciple; it may be presumed, all the most Admired Buildings which adorned that Imperial city, were but imitations of Grecian originals.

Although the Greek-Roman controversy had a long history in the eighteenth and nineteenth centuries, affecting the development of Greek and Roman revival architecture in western Europe and America and, through Winckelmann, influencing the course of German Classical scholarship, the greater success of the "Greek" party tended to downplay the aesthetic importance of the discoveries at Pompeii. Eventually, because of this and in the absence of the inflated reception given to the finds from Herculaneum, the excavations at Pompeii would be taken much more on their own terms without so much of an idealizing gloss. Still, Roman architecture, and Pompeian things, had their partisans: G. B. Piranesi took up the cudgels on behalf of Roman architectural genius and vitality in his *Della Magnificenza ed architettura de' Romani* (Rome, 1761) and the *Parera su l'architettura* (Rome, 1765). At the same time he went to Pompeii and drew many of the exposed ruins most sympathetically, including the newly famous *Temple of Isis*, discovered in 1765.

Piranesi's friend and admirer, the Scottish architect Robert Adam, was also a member of the "Roman" party, and played his part in the quarrel by publishing his *Ruins of the Palace of the Emperor Diocletian at Spalatro in Dalmatia* (London, 1764) and by employing Roman, even Pompeian motifs in his handsome decorative schemes for Kedleston Hall near Derby (1756–1768), Syon House in Middlesex (1762), the interior of Harewood House near Leeds (1760's), and Kenwood in London (1767–68). Even James "Athenian" Stuart succumbed to the Roman/Pompeian vogue of interior

The blue amphora shown here resembles in shape and size the Portland Vase which Sir William Hamilton purchased from a collector in Rome for the staggering price (for the time) of one thousand pounds and later resold to the dowager Duchess of Portland for nearly twice that amount. This look-alike was found in a tomb on the Street of Tombs outside the Herculaneum Gate and is an unusually ornate example of the cameo glass technique upon which Wedgwood's jasperware was based.

*Visitors view the excavation work at the Temple of Isis, an engraving by
Francesco Piranesi (son of Giambattista Piranesi) and Jean-Louis Després,
circa 1778–79.*

*Tomb of the priestess Mamia and the Street of Tombs, an engraving by
Francesco Piranesi and Jean-Louis Després, circa 1778–79.*

Excavation at the City Gate to Pompeii, an engraving by Francesco
Piranesi and Jean-Louis Després, 1778.

Excavation work at the Temple of Isis, a drawing by Giambattista Piranesi.

decoration in his design for the Painted Room at Spencer House in London (1759), while all over Winckelmann's Germany early nineteenth-century princely establishments had their "Pompeian" rooms with copies of paintings from Herculaneum, based on the *Antichità* plates, e.g. the Pompeian Room in Gotha Castle and in the Palais Brühl in Dresden, and Karl Friedrich Schinkel's 1825 design for the Pompeian Theater in Schloss Bertin for Frederick IV. English, French, and German artists and decorators adopted a mixed vocabulary of classical and neoclassical forms and images, culled from the great illustrated volumes of classical sites. Under the pressure of historicism and early romanticism these forms and images were transformed, often obscuring the original source, while imparting a classical flavor or sign to the composition. This process was initiated by Mengs and the French painter Joseph Marie Vien, a follower of Caylus and of Winckelmann and teacher of Jacques-Louis David, and continued especially through French and German academic painting until it reached the "correct" Alma-Tadema in the late nineteenth century. Occasionally, however, a classicizing artist might employ a specific antique model in recognizable form—so Robert Adam in his plan for the ground floor of 20 St James's Square in London (1772–74) which depends on the "typical" Pompeian town house.

Yet, gentle, neoclassical artists like Angelica Kauffmann, familiar with Winckelmann, Goethe, and Canova, had very little of ancient Pompeii in her touching painting of *The Younger Pliny and his Mother at Misenum, A.D. 79* (1785, Princeton University Museum). Similarly, the many artists who described the eruption of Mount Vesuvius on August 8, 1779, however mindful they were of the tragic event 1,700 years earlier, emphasized the contemporaneity of the extraordinary event. For them the past was still veiled, as it was for the poet Percy Bysshe Shelley who visited Pompeii in 1819 and wrote to his friend, Thomas Love Peacock, from Naples on January 19:

I was astonished at the remains of this city; I had no conception of anything so perfect remaining . . .

The day was radiant and warm. Every now and then we heard the subterranean thunder of Vesuvius; its distant deep peals seemed to shake the very air and light of day, which interpenetrated our frames, with the sullen and tremendous sound. This scene was what the Greeks beheld (Pompeii, you know, was a Greek city). They lived in harmony with

Drawing for a chimney piece, drafted by Robert Adam about 1775, from The Metropolitan Museum of Art.

nature; and the interstices of their incomparable columns were portals, as it were, to admit the spirit of beauty which animates this glorious universe to visit those whom it inspired. If such is Pompeii, what was Athens? What scene was exhibited from the Acropolis, the Parthenon, and the temples of Hercules, and Theseus, and the Winds? . . .

So wrote the poet, visitor to Pompeii after the first great period of its excavations but who saw the ruins through the hellenic veil, cast by Stuart and Revett and by Winckelmann. However, Pompeii had something that the antiquities of Athens could not match: not surface finds, not great blocks of stone strewn on the hard ground, not tumbled marble statues and reliefs, not isolated structures and things, but all of them, recovered in the excavation of a single ancient town, complete with all the apparatus of classical civilization. Such is the import of Sir William Hamilton's account of the recent discoveries at Pompeii, read to the Society of Antiquaries at London, January 26 and February 2 and 9, 1775, subsequently printed in the Society's journal, *Archaeologia* 4, 1777, pp. 160–175. Hamilton's report was accompanied by illustrations of the monuments discussed as they appeared after excavation and cleaning but without reconstruction, apart from an occasional plan. Typical of his thorough, if brief, treatment is this excerpt on the chapel of Isis whose importance he, as others, quickly recognized:

The walls of the cloisters, that were beautifully ornamented with arabesque paintings, most of which have been cut out, and carried to the Museum at Portici . . . Near the great altar . . . was a tablet of basalt, with Egyptian hieroglyphics engraved thereon, which has been carried to the Museum at Portici. Over the great gate of the Chapel was the following inscription in large characters, which has been likewise deposited in the Museum at Portici: (he then gives the inscription) . . . It is a pity that such monuments of antiquity as are not in immediate danger of suffering from the injuries of the weather, should have been removed from their places, where they would have afforded satisfaction and instruction to the curious who visit these antiquities . . . Many travellers have seen this chapel without knowing that it was certainly a chapel of Isis, and rebuilt by N. Popidius, after having been destroyed by an earthquake (in A.D. 62). The inscription, being now compounded with many others from Herculaneum and Stabiae, in the court of the Museum at Portici, may have easily escaped their notice . . . In another room was likewise found a skeleton with an iron crow lying near it. The paintings of the sides of this room, and even the brick wall, are much broken, probably by this person, who was inclosed by the cruel shower of pumice-stones and ashes that covered the city, and had been endeavoring, in vain, with the iron crow, to force his way out . . .

What then had been going on at Pompeii since the excavations were begun in 1748 under the direction of Alcubierre and Martorelli? Our knowledge is fragmentary

*Ever the enthusiastic amateur archaeologist, Sir William Hamilton was on
hand during the initial excavations at the Temple of Isis in 1765 (shown at
the site with British visitors in this illustration by Pietro Fabris from*
Campi Phlegraei*).*

and depends for the most part on two much later works for the period from 1748 to the
mid-nineteenth century—Giuseppe Fiorelli, *Pompeianarum Antiquitatum Historia*, Naples,
1860–1864, and August Mau, *Pompeii, its Life and Art*, translated by Francis W. Kelsey,
New York, 1899—and on the excavation reports themselves. Almost from the very
beginning of archaeological activity at Pompeii, the directors or superintendents (the
Soprastanti) maintained a journal on the course of the excavations, the *Giornale dei
Soprastanti*, which they sent to the General Superintendent in Naples; this practice has

continued to the present. Fiorelli edited the *Giornale* in Naples for the period 1748–1860. Until 1764 these reports consisted of lists of finds without classification and lacking any effort to describe the building or room in which objects were found. On the model of the Herculaneum publications, subject-paintings were usually described in detail without reference to the context of the room or the position of the panel in the decorative wall

Gold—in Pompeian days as now—was a coveted commodity for jewelry. The gold armband in the form of a serpent, one of a pair, was shaped from a flat ribbon of gold; a v-shaped punch was used to indicate the scales. The eight large loops of the gold bracelet were formed by two intertwining lengths of thick gold wire soldered together at each crossing. The necklace is composed of 48 ivy leaves stamped out of sheet gold and linked by gold wire loops. The clasp that joined the two concentric bands behind the neck is missing.

scheme. In 1765 the reports shift from Spanish to Italian; finds are then classified by material in decreasing order of value from gold to terra cotta and their provenance is given with slightly greater precision—at least the day of discovery of each group of finds is specified—but the significance of context remains unappreciated. Only in the early nineteenth century, and briefly at that, does there appear an effective interest in wall

This solid gold double-flame oil lamp created a sensation when it was discovered during the excavation work in 1863. The exquisitely crafted lotus leaves were worked in relief from the outside with a punch, as was the leaf-shaped reflector in front of the handle. The plain spouts and base were cast separately, then soldered into place. The lid, alas, was never found so we can only surmise that it must have matched the reflector in design. This lamp, probably produced in the early years of the Empire, is the most valuable ever uncovered in Pompeii.

Finding a skeleton in the baths, an engraving by Charles François Mazois.

schemes as a whole and in the context or ensemble of the panel pictures in a room; this interest quickly dies and slowly reappears in the 1850's. Not only are the lists difficult to use, but, as William Hamilton observed, the objects often were mixed up with others coming from Herculaneum and Stabiae once they arrived in the Museum at Portici, and even more so when the museum was moved to Naples in 1787.

Even limited confidence in the value and accuracy of these lists is severely tested by the many stories about the marvelous "discoveries" made for royal visitors, and right in front of their eyes at that. On April 7, 1769 the King of the Two Sicilies, Ferdinand IV ("Big Nose"); his queen, Caroline, daughter of Maria Theresa of Austria; the Emperor Joseph II; Count Kaunitz; William Hamilton; and M. d'Ancrevil visited Pompeii. The finds for the day were so rich that the emperor thought that the objects had been planted for his benefit, until Hamilton and the chief of excavations, Francesco La Vega, convinced him otherwise. But the same charade was played out for Joseph Bonaparte and his consort early in the nineteenth century, for Murat and his wife, Caroline—who liked to find skeletons decked out in jewelry—and for many other distinguished visitors. Typical of the privileges extended to noble titles is the experience of the Duke of Bedford who visited Pompeii in the spring of 1815 and was presented with a bronze satyr, just excavated before him, by Queen Caroline; the satyr is now in Woburn Abbey.[3] But aristocratic patronage was needed to finance the excavations, and the thrill of discovery made them generous. The tradition of mining an archaeological site for its treasures died hard.

Still, great progress was made and it is worthwhile to record the salient developments in the early history of the excavations of Pompeii. By these means the monuments became known, the typology of the town house emerged, consciousness of the street network and its meaning was aroused, and ever so slowly the city and all its parts appeared in comprehensible form. But beyond itself, Pompeii established the prime model for the subsequent excavation of the classical sites of the Mediterranean basin, even if such excavations would wait more than a century for their own beginnings. Thus, the history of the excavations of Pompeii is an essential part of the history of archaeology as an art, a science, and a discipline.

1748

Excavation begun at Pompeii on the *Via di Nola*, on the *Street of Tombs* near the *Herculaneum Gate*, and on part of the *Amphitheater*.

1750

Work suspended because little of interest (e.g. treasure) found.

1754

Excavation resumed with the discovery of more tombs; the *Villas of Julia Felix* and *of Cicero* excavated but reburied; buildings were named according to inscriptions found in them or near them, by the presence of striking works of art or of objects, by peculiarities of form, and by guesswork, sometimes even for honored guests or for state occasions.

1763

Discovery of the inscription of Suedius Clemens proving that Città was Pompeii; from this time excavated areas were left uncovered, and unprotected; conservation not considered because the precious objects, including paintings, inscriptions, furniture and utensils, were removed.

Nothing could look more serene than the Amphitheater as it appears today,
its seats grown over with grass and the arena floor more resembling a part of
a golf course than a place of combat.

Niccolini reconstructions of gladiatorial attire and Amphitheater decor.

Inside the Amphitheater—struggle for supremacy (and survival) between beasts and brawny gladiators (a Niccolini reconstruction).

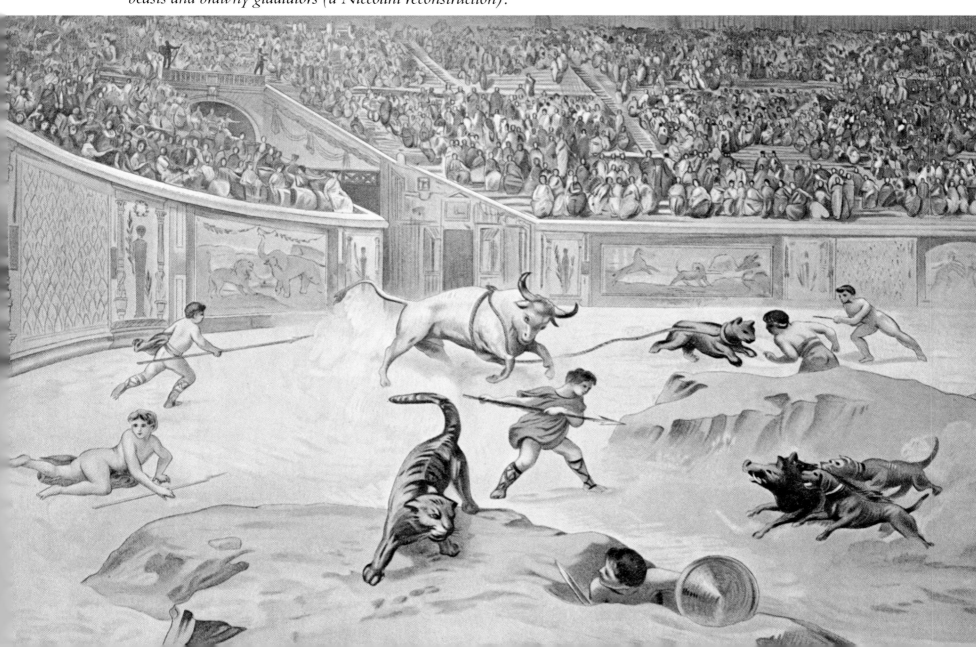

Chief entrance to the arena at the Amphitheater.

Arches and external steps of the Amphitheater.

Two of the most-reproduced wall paintings from the Villa of Cicero, here shown as painted by Wilhelm Zahn. Both depict maenads riding centaurs and with two other similar paintings may have been part of a clear-cut continuous frieze at one time. Both popular and widely publicized, these maenad/centaur paintings adorned porcelain and panels, inlays and plasterwork throughout the neoclassic and Empire periods.

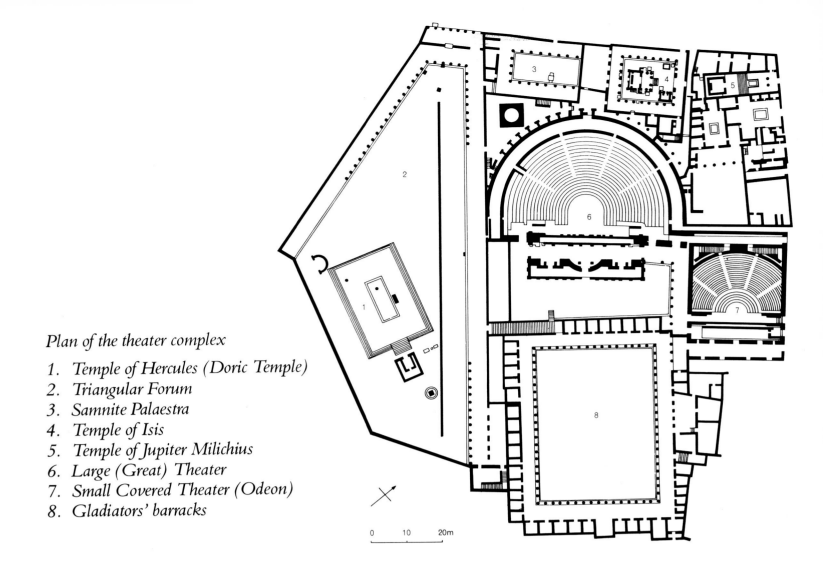

Plan of the theater complex

1. Temple of Hercules (Doric Temple)
2. Triangular Forum
3. Samnite Palaestra
4. Temple of Isis
5. Temple of Jupiter Milichius
6. Large (Great) Theater
7. Small Covered Theater (Odeon)
8. Gladiators' barracks

0   10   20m

East portico of the Triangular Forum
from the south. The Ionic-columned
atrium in the rear was the entrance,
but the columns of the portico are an
advanced Doric form.

80

The Large (or Great) Theater at Pompeii, an engraving by G. Hackert from a 1793 drawing by J. Philipp Hackert.

Inside the Odeon (Small Theater).

81

*A view of the ongoing construction work at the Temple of Isis, an engraving
from a drawing by Jean-Louis Després in 1779 included in* Picturesque
Voyage to Naples and to Sicily.

1764
Excavation of the *Triangular Forum*, of the *Porticus*, the *Large Theater*, the *Odeon*, and the
so-called "*Quartiere*" (the large rectangular, porticated courtyard behind the theater)
begun and continued sporadically until circa 1800 when entire area was finally cleared;
many corpses found in the porticated court and much gladiatorial armor.

1765

Work on the *Temple of Isis* complex begun in December 1764 and continued until October 1766; immediately recognized as a major find.

1760's

Until circa 1800 excavation continued on the *Street of Tombs* (Strada dei Sepolcri) and the area of the *Herculaneum Gate*, including the *Tomb of Mamia*, and on the *Insula Occidentale* (then known as the Podere di Irace) on the western edge of town.

The Necropolis outside the Herculaneum Gate (south side of the road). The tombs of Aulus Veius (left) and the priestess Mamia, both boasting semicircular stone seats, flank the façade of the Tomb of Marcus Porcius backed by a mausoleum once topped by an open-air round temple. The 19th-century strollers were supplied by Niccolini.

*View of the new discoveries in the Insula Occidentale, an engraving from a
drawing by Charles François Mazois.*

1771

Work begun on the *Villa of Diomedes* to the west of the Villa of Cicero and on the *House
of the Surgeon* (Casa del Chirurgo), so-called from surgical instruments found there; in
December 1772 18 bodies and the imprint of a handsome bosom were discovered in the
Villa of Diomedes; although the system of classification of areas in Pompeii according to
regiones and *insulae* (blocks) and doorways was not developed until Fiorelli's
administration in the 1860's; houses will then be located by their regionary catalogue
number, thus the House of the Surgeon is VI-1-9.10.

1778

Francesco La Vega became director of the excavations until 1797 and developed the first
plan of the site.

1787

Museum moved from Portici to Naples.

In order to protect the priceless artifacts and antiquities of Pompeii and Herculaneum from the continued volcanic activity of Vesuvius, the Naples Museum was refurbished to house them. In 1787, amid a cheering populace, the great equestrian statues and treasures were conveyed on wheeled carriers made especially for this purpose in a lengthy convoy under the observation of the king and queen (in the box) to their new home (an engraving by Francesco Piranesi and Jean-Louis Després).

1798

The French occupied the kingdom of Naples; work begun on the *House of Championnet* (VII-2-1.3), named after the commander of the French troops; progress slowed down until the advent of Murat in 1807.

1808

House of Polybius (VI occ. 23–26) excavated.

An etching of the restoration work at the
House of Sallust.

Plan of the House of Sallust

1809
Work resumed on the House of Championnet and other houses near the Forum (VII-2-1.3), including the *House of Actaeon* (Casa di Atteone, VI-2-4), now called the *House of Sallust.*
1813
Area around House of Championnet cleared, also portico of the Theater, area around *Amphitheater*; the *Basilica* began to emerge at the southwest corner of the Forum.
1814
Work on Basilica and amphitheater intensified.

86

Inside the Basilica. Never reconstructed after the earthquake, the cut-off columns of the Basilica resemble tree stumps in a uniform row. "Basilica" was scratched in several places on the remains, and the general shape is that used in similar edifices in later times.

Temple of Apollo. Badly damaged in the earthquake in A.D. 62, the temple was quickly restored but unfortunately not in the classic likeness of old. A good many Roman frills were added including stucco in garish colors. The inscription on the altar tells us the restoration was commissioned by a decree of the council.

*West portico of the Forum from within.
The two-tiered colonnade was composed
of a sturdy Doric story on the bottom
supporting the upper Ionic columns.*

Plan of the Forum

1. Temple of Jupiter
2. Macellum (provisions market)
3. Sanctuary of the City Lares
4. Temple of Vespasian
5. Building of Eumachia (fullers hall)
6. Comitium (voting hall)
7. Duovirs' (chief magistrates') office
8. Council chamber
9. Aediles' (junior magistrates') office
10. Basilica
11. Temple of Apollo
12. Control of weights and measures
13. Cereals market
14. Commemorative arches

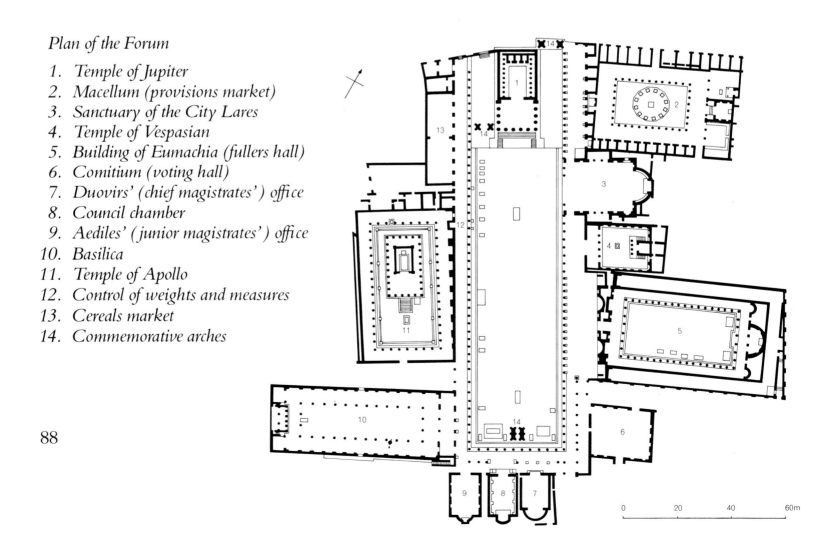

An engraving of excavation work at the Forum by Charles François Mazois.

1816

Clearing of area around the *Basilica* extended into the *Forum* and actively continued until 1820; in *1817* the beginning of the *Via dell'Abbondanza* (the Street of Abundance) was opened at the edge of the Forum; *1818* work begun on the large temple on the west side of the Forum, then believed to be a temple of Venus but now known as the *Temple of Apollo* (VII–8–31.32).

1816

Museo Reale Borbonico established in Naples to house the growing finds from Pompeii and the older material, once kept at Portici.

1819

Street leading to theaters cleared, and possibly also some houses in area of the *Stabian Gate*; area around the so-called "chalcidicum," the vestibule of the Basilica, and the *Basilica* itself now sufficiently cleared for a plan to be drawn (by Bonucci).

1820

Clearing of the *Forum* continued; the clearing of the *Building of Eumachia* on the southeastern side of the Forum at the Corner of the Via dell'Abbondanza begun.

1817/19

The first edition of *Pompeiana: The Topography, Edifices, and Ornaments of Pompeii* by William Gell, with engravings by J. P. Gandy appeared in London (see *Exploitation*).

Portal of the Building of Eumachia. The frame with a picturesque pattern of leaves and animals was fitted into a larger portal after the earthquake by way of further reinforcement.

90

Although the actual statue of Eumachia now resides in the Naples Museum, Sir William Gell drew it in its original position and wrote: "The place [where the statue is located] may be styled rather a recess than a niche, and the statue being found on the spot, becomes an object of peculiar interest and importance."

The Priestess Eumachia, a marble statue found in the Building of Eumachia, erected in her honor by the fullers guild, is in a remarkable state of preservation, and from the remaining paint there is strong evidence that she was a redhead.

The Temple of Isis, pictured in ruins as Niccolini saw it here, must have been memorable before the eruption. Reached by a flight of ten steps, the sanctuary was graced by splendid Doric columns with red and white shafts. Egyptian overtones abound—even the candelabra were in lotus shapes.

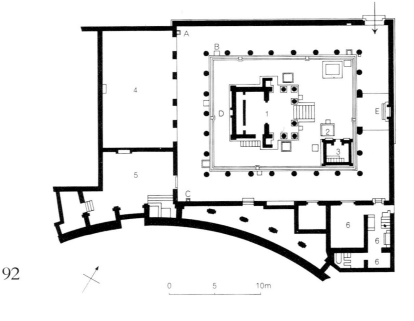

Plan of the Temple of Isis

1. Temple
2. Main altar
3. Building with water tank
4. Meeting hall
5. Initiation chamber
6. Priests' lodging

A. Statue of Venus
B. Statue of Isis
C. Herm of Norbanus Sorex
D. Statue of Dionysus
E. Shrine of Harpocrates

0   5   10m

Marble statue of Isis found in the northwest corner of the colonnade in the Temple of Isis. Her long, form-fitting tunic is gathered under her breasts by a clasp composed of the heads of two serpents, while her elaborately coiffed hair is crowned by rosettes. The original coloring of the statue has long since disappeared, but the Niccolini reconstruction presented shows the rich red embellishments that adorned it when first found. The base on which the statue stands bears some indication that the Temple of Isis was official municipal property.

A somewhat restored Temple of Isis, an engraving by Charles François Mazois.

A Ceremony of the Cult of Isis (or The Adoration of the Sacred Water), a wall painting found in Herculaneum—proof positive that Isis rites were performed in Herculaneum even though no temple has been found there to date. The painting represents a ceremony where the high priest, with shaven head and wearing a linen vestment, raises a vase containing the sacred water of the Nile—a symbol of the productive forces of Nature—under the figure of the Nile that fertilizes Egypt before the faithful who line the stairs. An altar on which perfumes and offerings are burning stands at the foot of the temple steps, and a priest fans the sacred fire while musicians play the flute and onlookers shake the sistra.

Isis was first and foremost the patron goddess of navigation, and certain ceremonies highlighted this aspect of her powers. One of the most curious of these was the Feast of the Ship of Isis, held on March 15 and extremely popular all along the shores of the Mediterranean. There was a procession from the Isium (temple) to the seashore; then all the ships that had been stranded and afterwards brought ashore during the past year were—with suitable fanfare—launched on the sea again.

A new ship was also sent to sea on the same day, as a sign that the season of navigation had begun again. Certain paintings in the Temple of Isis represented ships thus offered to the goddess, whose name they bore. (Both the portrayal of the Feast and a cutter christened Isis were reconstructed by Fausto Niccolini.)

The sistrum (plural sistra) used in the Isis rites was an Egyptian religious instrument (Isis took it over from Hathor, the Egyptian goddess of music), the round part of which represented the world, according to Plutarch, and the four-cross-rods the four elements. The sistrum, when shaken, was supposed to be a symbol of the eternal movement of nature, instrumental in repelling the forces of evil and also to express joy or mourning.

Io Landing in Egypt, a wall painting found in the Temple of Isis in the large assembly room to the rear, reportedly represents Io, borne on the shoulders of Nilus (a water god), landing in Egypt and welcomed by Isis, ensconced on a rock and holding the uraeus (sacred serpent) in her hand with her small son by her side. Mythology has it that Io was turned into a cow by Hera because Zeus loved her, and that in this state she was driven from one country to another until she finally found rest in Egypt and subsequently gave birth to Zeus's son who went on to become king of Egypt.

The vision of the whole was beginning to form, and with it a growing sense of the miraculous nature of the discovery which joined past and present together. Significantly, the excavation of Pompeii, which left more and more of the city uncovered and thus exposed more completely than ever before the texture of urban life in Antiquity, made it possible for historians of the ancient world to conceive of the patterns of daily life and of the physical environments developed for them. If on one hand this led eventually to the creation of a well-founded social history of Roman (or Pompeian) life, to the growth of archaeology as a valid technique of historical research, and to the enrichment of the history of Roman architecture, the image of Pompeii reborn and of the Pompeians revisited struck the poets with romantic force. So Schiller's poem:

Pompeii and Herculaneum

What miracle is this? We pray for springs to quench our thirst
Of thee, O Earth! what gifts are these thy silent womb has nursed?
Does life yet stir in the abyss? Beneath the Lava plain
Dwells a race concealed?—returns the Past to life again?
Greeks! Romans! come—oh see! Pompeii's ancient wall behold
Restored anew! Herculean towers again their pride unfold.
Roof over roof ascends—the spacious Portico spreads wide
Its arch—Oh hither haste, to swell the people's rushing tide!
The Theater its doors expands—its seven wide mouths invite
The expectant crowd fast pouring in to view the gala . . .

. . . .

The cleanly streets stretch far and wide—the narrow footpaths, flanked
With silent dwellings, wind along, on causeways high embanked.
The roofs, for shelter formed and shade—the chambers fair to see
That range along the lonely court in social privacy.
Quick! open wide the shutters—bid the long-closed gates give way,
And on the night of ages pour the vivid flood of day!

. . . .

—There's nothing lost. Earth yet hath kept her trust right faithfully.[4]

*View from the roof of the thermae, an engraving from a sketch by Sir
William Gell.*

Exploitation
The City of the Dead and for the Living, 1820–1880

S IR William Gell's *Pompeiana: The Topography, Edifices and Ornaments of Pompeii, The Result of Excavations since 1819* (2 volumes, London, 1832) opens with a lengthy preface which clearly spells out the benefits and hazards of the new excavations:

The favorable manner in which the former part of this work was received by the Public has been sufficiently demonstrated by the extensive circulation and rapid sale of the two editions, which seem to have found their way, not only to every part of Great Britain, but even to the Continent, where the collection of Pompeiana has been noticed with approbation in many of the literary journals . . . Among (the recent discoveries), the excavation of the Chalcidicum, which took place soon after the publication of the former work, laid open the only example of that species of edifice which has existed in modern times. Not long afterwards, the great area of the Pantheon was discovered, and the whole circuit of the Forum was perfectly cleared . . . an entrance was opened into an area which proved to belong to the public baths or Thermae of the city. Some of the apartments of this edifice yet remained covered by stone arches, which, having resisted the pressure of the cinders and accumulated fresh earth, retained, in all their original freshness of colour, those beautiful ornaments and fretted ceilings, of which so few have resisted the lapse of eighteen centuries. The discovery of the baths is perhaps of greater consequence than may at first appear, for, notwithstanding the enormous ruins of the Roman Thermae, their component parts seem to have been little understood, and even variously named by the authors who have undertaken their elucidation. At Pompeii, on the contrary, the absence of Xystus, Theater, Palaestra, and an infinite number of other intricate divisions which render the Thermae of the great Capital so complicated and unintelligible, leaves a satisfactory and defined idea of the use and meaning of every other portion of the fabric . . . These various objects, with the house named that of the Tragic Poet, situated opposite to the northern side of the Thermae, cover a plot of ground advancing nearer to the center of Pompeii than any which had been formerly cleared, and, in consequence of a greater depth of superincumbent soil, they have, generally, been found in a better state of preservation. They form, altogether, the connexion of two portions of the plan of the city, which were scarcely united by the unfinished excavation of the Forum . . . The house of the Tragic Poet has exhibited superior specimens of painting, while the subject of ancient art itself is exciting more of the public attention, and meeting with merited though tardy admiration. . . .

With such an accession of new materials, the Author of the present work has thought it advisable to lay them before the public without delay, aware that time will incalculably diminish the freshness of those objects, which, when stripped of their external coats by the rains of winter or the burning suns of summer, lose by far the greater portion of their interest and identity. Another motive for the immediate publication of whatever can be collected is the great and increasing difficulty of obtaining permission to draw and measure the newly discovered antiquities, by which a foreigner is reduced to snatch from eternal oblivion only such morsels as a favorable moment may enable him to delineate. An astonishing number of interesting objects is annually and hourly destroyed by the action of weather upon substances and surfaces which have been once subjected to the operation of heat and moisture; and this unavoidable delay is more to be lamented, as strangers are seldom allowed to draw until the decomposition both of colour and substance has taken place to a great extent; while,

100

Frigidarium and piscina in the women's baths, an engraving from a sketch by Sir William Gell.

even if they were delineated by a native artist, there are no engravers on the spot of sufficient skill to multiply the copies, nor a public sufficiently educated to encourage the sale of them. An instance of the delay which takes place in the native publications may be observed in the description of the Temple of Isis, which, though discovered at so early a period (1765), is only at this moment in the progress of illustration by the care of the Cavaliere Carelli, whose elaborate account of that interesting relic, with drawings made at the time of the excavation, is only now in preparation; while the monument itself has already lost the last vestiges of the beauty and freshness in which it first appeared . . . At the present moment, in the year 1826, only those parts of Pompeii can be drawn and measured with the consent of those immediately concerned, which have been discovered prior to the year 1823 . . . A foreign antiquary can only hope for better times and a more liberal policy with regard to Pompeii. . . .

. . . .

It may not be quite uninteresting to notice the progress of the excavations, which, notwithstanding all that has been said on the subject to the contrary, seem to have been as well conducted, and as steadily pursued, as times and circumstances have permitted . . . and, though, it be true that more labourers might have been employed, it is not less so that the work ought not to proceed till the objects already explored are roofed and fortified against the weather. At present, considerable expense attends the excavation . . . The preservation of the vaults of the Thermae has been a work of no trifling importance . . . The merit of Signor Bonucci the elder has been conspicuous on these occasions, and it is to be hoped that his successor may continue the system. The director is assisted by an intendant, who is on the spot, and by three overseers, who not only watch the workmen but sometimes show objects of particular interest to travellers. In addition to these, is a number of inferior custodi or guardians, whose chief duties consist in accompanying visitors, or taking care of such ruins as, being considered of more importance, are shut up from the vulgar by way of protection from wanton injury, or the inscription of names by which many beautiful relics have suffered. It is usual for travellers to bestow a trifle upon the custodi. . . .

. . . .

It has been the custom to honour the arrival of illustrious personages by excavating in their presence some small portion of Pompeii; an enviable method of showing respect exclusively possessed by the court of Naples. For these occasions, an order is given that the earth should be left undisturbed to the depth of a foot or more, in several of the rooms of a newly discovered house, and, on the day appointed, these are cleared out for the amusement of the guests. It is seldom a fruitless search . . . Not a day passes without the discovery of something of greater or less importance . . .

It may be observed that nearly the whole of the objects detailed in this work might have passed away without representation or record, had not the Author been on the spot, and thus been enabled to avail himself of every favorable moment for acquiring the necessary materials for this work. . . .

Street of the Mercuries, an engraving from a sketch by Sir William Gell.

View of the court of the piscina, House of the Dioscuri [Castor and Pollux],
an engraving from a sketch by Sir William Gell.

Wall and door of the Corinthian peristyle, House of the Dioscuri [Castor and Pollux], an engraving from a sketch by Sir William Gell.

Despite Gell's complaints, which will echo for more than a century, a great deal was achieved by the excavators of Pompeii in the period from 1820 to 1880. Although this sixty-year period is somewhat artificially defined, it does possess certain legitimate boundaries, stretching from the restoration of the Bourbon monarchy and the development of the area around the Forum to the active regime of Michele Ruggiero as director, his institution of modern methods of restoration, and the appearance of monographic studies on Pompeian topics by Italian and foreign writers, most notably August Mau. The watershed between collection and scientific analysis occurred during the revolutionary directorship of Giuseppe Fiorelli, beginning in 1860, who changed forever the character of archaeology at Pompeii; he imposed systematic controls over the acquisition, recording, classification, and publication of information gathered from excavations and study. In doing so he not only brought order to the continuing archaeological enterprise at Pompeii but also offered a model for other excavations in the Classical world of the Mediterranean.

Information about the course of the excavations in this period comes from the excavators' reports, many of them correlated and published by Fiorelli or Mau, either in the form of retrospective accounts on the activities of several years' work or in more descriptive notices of current activity. From these materials patterns of innovation in archaeological techniques emerge, as well as the appearance of a greater range of objectives in excavation and research, that justify a further division of this sixty-year period into three parts: 1820–1848, 1850–1859, 1860–1880.

1821

Work begun on the north and east sides of the *Forum* and along the *Strada del Foro*; this

Gate of Isis [commonly called that of Nola], an engraving from a sketch by Sir William Gell.

work continued until *1824*, shops appeared, and in *1822* the *Macellum* or market was discovered on the northeastern edge of the Forum.

1824

The *Temple of Fortuna Augusta* (VII-4-1) was found, work begun on the *Strada di Nola*, located northeast of the Forum and running to the *Nolan Gate*; at this time the street was called the *Strada di Fortuna*.

The *Forum Baths* were discovered and partially excavated during the summer months; in December work on the soon-to-be famous *House of the Tragic Poet* (VI-8-5) was begun and continued for the next two years.

Antonio Niccolini began publishing the *Real Museo Borbonico* (16 volumes, Naples, 1824–1857) which consisted of an old-style catalogue of the holdings (mostly ancient) of the Naples Museum and, at the end, a brief account of current excavations at Pompeii. Charles François Mazois published the first volume of his sumptuously illustrated *Les Ruines de Pompéi* (4 volumes, Paris, 1824–1838).

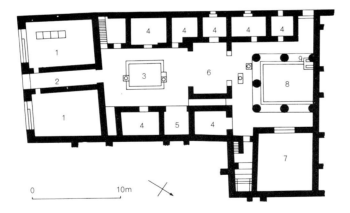

Plan of the House of the Tragic Poet

1. *Shops*
2. *Fauces (corridors)*
3. *Atrium (central meeting room)*
4. *Bedrooms (cubicula)*
5. *Ala (back room recesses)*
6. *Tablinum (usually the master's office)*
7. *Oecus (living room)*
8. *Peristyle garden (colonnaded courtyar*
9. *Lararium (shrine to household gods)*

Mosaic watchdog and other decor details from the House of the Tragic Poet (a Niccolini reconstruction).

107

Wall painting of the nuptials of Zeus and Hera, from the House of the
Tragic Poet. Zeus sits to the right, while Hypnos performs the introduction
to a reluctant Hera. The scene is Mount Ida, and some of the smaller figures
have Cybeline overtones (a Niccolini reconstruction).

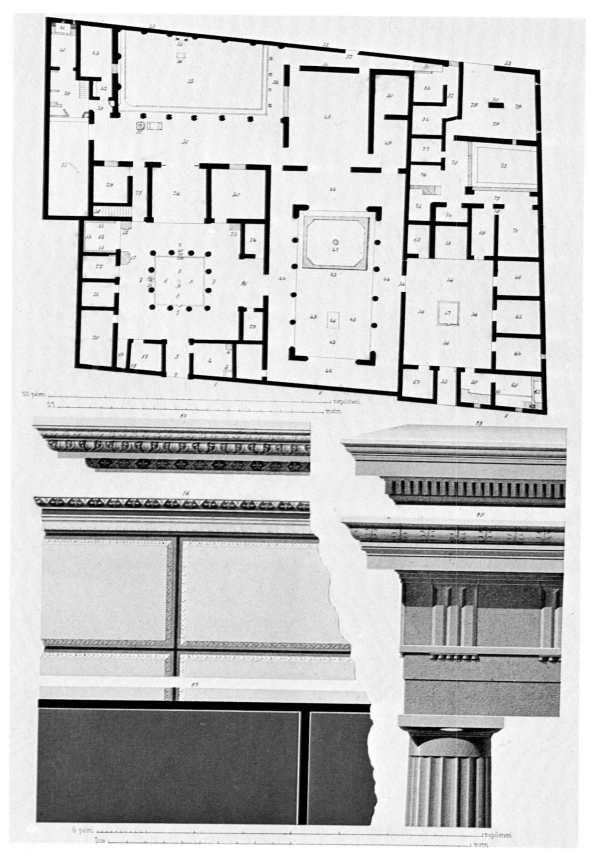

House plan, capital of column and detail of wall decor from the House of Castor and Pollux (a Niccolini reconstruction).

109

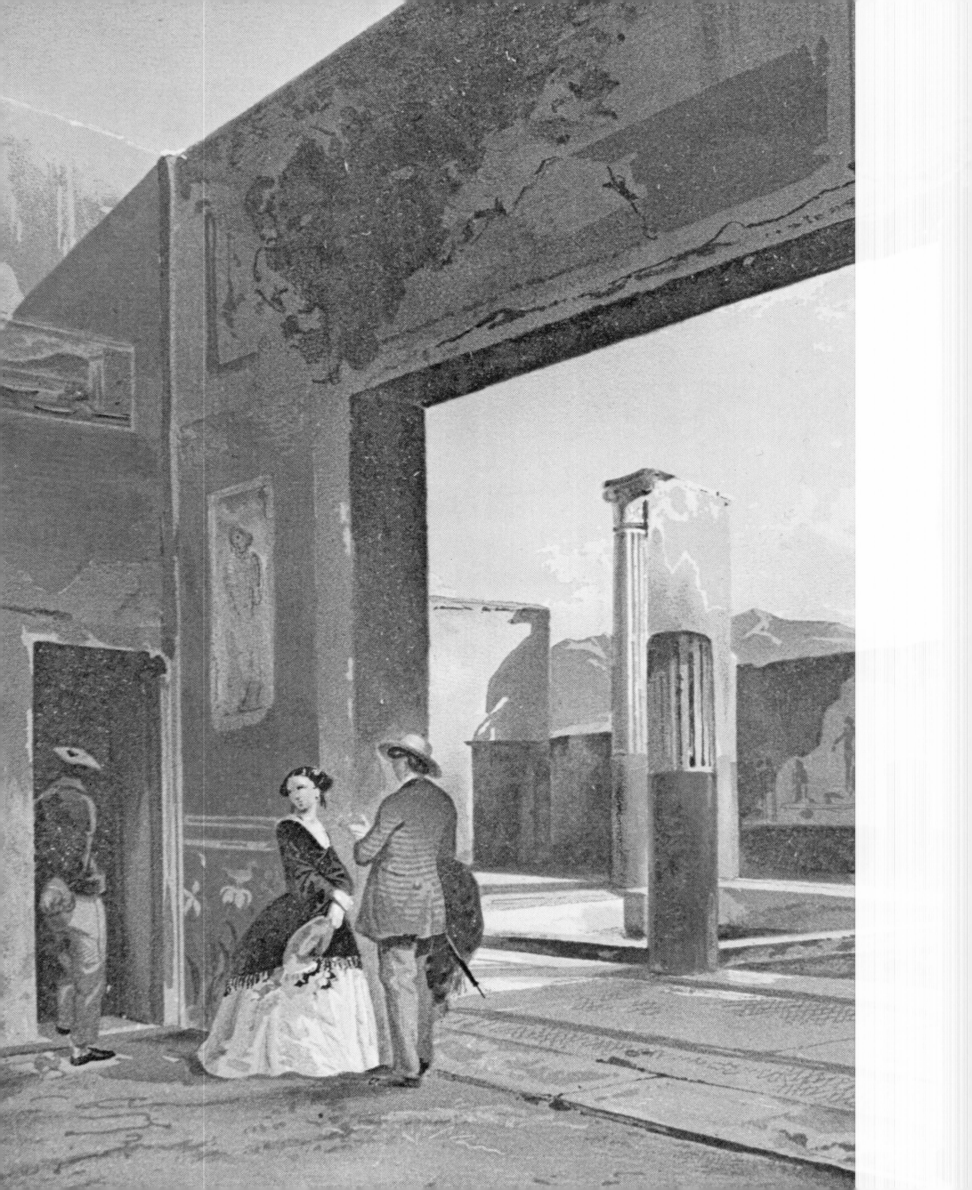

A visiting couple pauses in the archway of the House of Castor and Pollux
(by Niccolini).

1825

On July 2 arch discovered over entrance of the street continuing the line northward of the Strada del Foro, here the *Strada di Mercurio*; excavation followed street, and fullery discovered (VI-8-20).

1826

Work continued along the Strada di Mercurio, *House of the Great Fountain* (VI-8-22) discovered.

Leopold I of Belgium visited Pompeii.

1827

The *House of the Small Fountain* (VI-8-23), next along the Strada di Mercurio, was found; work resumed on the rear of the *House of Pansa* (VI-6-1), on the center of the Forum, and on the amphitheater.

Detailed map of all exposed areas of Pompeii undertaken by M. Bibent; semi-popular guide-book to Pompeii published by Carlo Bonucci, the first of many editions.

1828

Work continued along the Strada di Mercurio; excavation begun on the *House of Castor and Pollux* (the Dioscuri) (VI-9-6).

1829

Excavation of the *House of Castor and Pollux* completed by May; pace quickened as *Houses of the Centaur* (VI-9-3) and *of Meleager* (VI-9-2) were opened.

The memorable mosaic masterpiece showing Alexander the Great fighting Darius and the Persians in the Battle of Issus was discovered on the floor of the exedra in the House of the Faun in 1831. Investigation indicated that the severe damage to one corner took place prior to A.D. 79, possibly during the earlier earthquake. The entire panoramic work contains over a million and a half small stones. Considered too valuable to be left in position, it was cut out of the floor and taken to the museum in Naples.

1829

Ludwig of Bavaria visited Pompeii.

The German Archaeological Institute was founded as a private institution of international scope, under the name of *Istituto di corrispondenza archeologica* with its seat in Rome; began to issue the *Bollettino dell'Istituto di Corrispondenza Archeologica* as an annual with articles on Pompeii, excavations and analysis, from the very beginning; soon had very wide circulation.

1830

Work continued on the *House of Meleager* and on houses on the opposite side of the Strada di Mercurio.

House of the Faun discovered (VI-12-2/5); excavations proceeded from the street inward reaching the garden, peristyle, and servants quarters by *1832*; on *October 24, 1831* the *Alexander Mosaic* was uncovered and remained in place, protected by a lean-to until September *1843* when it was removed to the Real Museum in Naples. Goethe responded with enormous enthusiasm to the news of the Alexander Mosaic.

No attempt was made in the rendering of Alexander to enhance his appearance or glorify the battle conditions. Intent on the proceedings, he rides forward on his horse; one of his officers can be glimpsed in the background.

Each detail of the mosaic is meticulous. In this detail of Darius on his battle chariot, the golden band around his neck, the chariot mountings and his Persian attire have been painstakingly reproduced.

The exedra in which the mosaic was found was a bright and open place, truly lovely in concept, affording two attractive vistas—one of the expansive garden and its colonnades and the other of the smaller peristyle court.

116

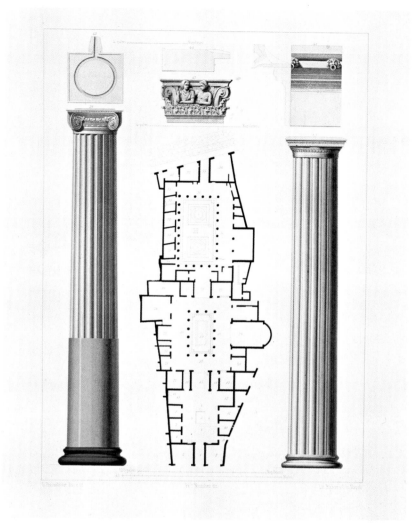

House plan and column reconstructions,
House of the Colored [Painted] Capitals
(by Niccolini).

1832

Three houses on the Strada della Fortuna opposite the House of the Faun were excavated including the *House of the Figured Capitals* (VII–4–57) and the *House of the Grand Duke of Tuscany*; off the *Strada degli Augustali*, work begun on the *House of the Painted Capitals* (VII–4–51).

Gell's *Pompeiana* was published.

1833
Excavation continued in the House of the Painted Capitals and on the Strada della Fortuna, including the *House of the Hunt* (VII-4-48).

1834
Clearing operations along the *Strada della Fortuna* and the *Vico Storto* and other alleyways continued for several years; *House of the Labyrinth* (VI-11-10) begun.

1835
House of Apollo begun (VI-7-23) and neighboring houses.

1836
Vico della Fullonica (VI-7) was partly opened.

1837
Extensive work continued on the *Strada dell'Abbondanza* (then called the *Strada dei Mercanti*, or "Shop Street") for the next three years.

1834–1842
Work continued in regions VI, VII, and VIII along several streets—*Strada della Fortuna, Vico della Fullonica, Strada dell'Abbondanza, Strada di Mercurio*—and on side streets dependent on them; areas around many of the individually excavated houses now enlarged and slowly coalescing; *House of the Boar* opened (VIII-3-8).

1843–1849
Excavations intensified in regions VI and VII, on the *Strada della Fortuna*, the *Strada di Nola*, and the *Strada Stabiana* (then called the *Strada del Quadrivio*), including the *House of the New Hunt* (VII-10-3.14), the *House of Orpheus* (VI-14-20, now called the *House of M. Vesonius Primus*), and several shops. In 1849 work suspended.

*View of the Colored Capitals for which the h[ouse]
named (by Niccolini).*

118

This scene of a dancing maenad and satyr separated by a small shrine was discovered in the tablinum of the House of the Colored Capitals. The figures are composed of colored marble pieces, shaped and inlaid on the black background in a technique known as intarsia.

1847

Edward Falkener conducted a private excavation of the *House of Marcus Lucretius* (IX- 3-5), begun on March 17 and terminating at the end of June; permission to excavate a house was granted by Marchese Santangelo, the Bourbon Minister of the Interior, and Falkener himself made the selection and "attended the excavations several times a day, watching nearly every morsel of stone, stucco, or charcoal that was turned up." [1]

1848

Publication of *Bollettino Archaeologico Napoletano* begun.

1849

In October Pope Pius IX visited Pompeii.

During the period 1820–1850, an apparently haphazard choice of sites was gradually rationalized as the street network became the guideline for progressive excavation. Consistent with this natural development, the excavators exhibited an interest in uncovering areas that could be comprehended as neighborhoods or districts. Although the significance of the street network was not fully appreciated, when the *Strada di Mercurio* was fully uncovered in 1830 the reports described it as a major artery from the Forum to the walls, leading to the gate that led out to the suburban villas outside the walls; the Strada di Mercurio and the *Strada della Fortuna* were dug down to the street surface about 1840, thus providing a more secure understanding of the full elevations of the adjoining houses. Plans of houses, excavated and cleared, were carefully made but not described or analyzed in detail. There were a few exceptions: for the

*Fountain niche in the garden of the
House of Marcus Lucretius.*

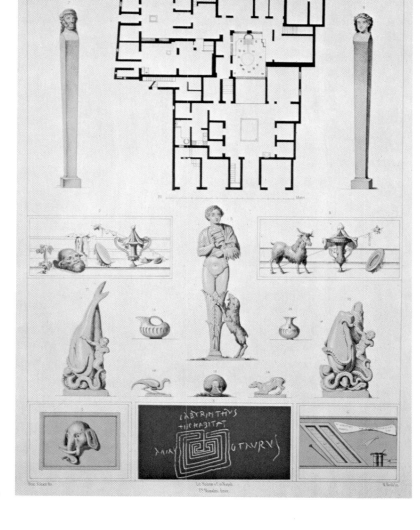

*House plan and decorative details of the
House of Marcus Lucretius (by Niccolini).*

House of the Faun the back area of garden and peristyle was studied with speculation on the function of various rooms, the garden and Corinthian oecus of the House of Meleager were similarly treated, while the House of the Tragic Poet and its adjoining fullery got a closely detailed discussion with measurements, references to building techniques, and a description of the operations of the fullery. Some buildings were misunderstood, such as the *Macellum* or Forum Market which was called the *Pantheon* at this time, and the implications of others, such as bath buildings, were inadequately appreciated despite careful plans.

Finds still took up the majority of each report, usually catalogued by day of discovery (or week, or longer) with a provenance. In the manner of the Herculaneum reports, works of art, and especially paintings, received the most thorough treatment; subject paintings, e.g. panels, were fully described and their location in a house specified, but their role in the decorative scheme of a painted wall almost completely ignored. Mosaics were similarly treated in isolation, although the quality of the Alexander Mosaic in the House of the Faun drew special attention. Statuary was listed with other finds, divided according to material, much as the Elder Pliny had done in his encyclopedic *Natural History*, while utensils and tools were often lumped together. Human remains,

121

however, took first place; the exact location of the find was given, especially when the skeleton was associated with jewelry or precious objects, and there was evidence of a respect for the dead, lost under the most dramatic circumstances. From the find lists, it is evident that most movable objects were intended for the Royal Museum in Naples, while some objects of minor value might be given directly to distinguished visitors for their collections, or as a memento of the occasion. And yet, treatment of the finds and of the excavations was anything but cavalier; in the entry for March 28–June, 1828, the excavator remarks on the breadth of information to be drawn from the site, comparing it to a book which cannot be closed, so varied and fascinating its contents.

The head of Apollo the Citharist (the name given to the house in which the statue was found). The hair is rolled round a circlet which confines the head and falls in a fringe of curls. The face with its large silver eyes has an enigmatic expression in keeping with the character of Apollo, the god of prophecy. Not visible here but still of interest, the statue's right hand still holds a plectrum *but the* cithara *(lyre) on which to use it has vanished.*

1850

Work resumed with clearing of city walls, beginning in the area of the *Porta Marina*, and on the *Strada Stabiana*, as well as on the long street from the *Temple of Isis* towards the amphitheater; continued for most of the decade.

1854

Large building at the intersection of the Strada Stabiana and the Strada dell'Abbondanza emerged and by April was identified as the *Stabian Baths*; work continued there for almost five years.

1858

One of the largest and most splendid of all Pompeii's houses was found, the *House of the Citharist* (I-4-5), named for the statue of *Apollo the Citharist* discovered therein; the elegant panel pictures were stripped from the walls.

1860

Work suspended again with the fall of the Bourbon dynasty in the face of Garibaldi's march; Alexandre Dumas' brief role as "director."

The Real Museo Borbonico was converted into the Museo Nazionale, as Naples was incorporated into the Kingdom of Italy.

Giuseppe Fiorelli became director of excavations and he published *Pompeianarum antiquitatum historia* (Naples, 1860/64), the first definitive history of the excavations of Pompeii.

For the most part, the reports of this decade followed the pattern of the earlier 1820–1850 period with two major shifts in treatment. Although there was no thorough discussion of the street network, the reports reflected an increasing sensitivity to the direction of streets and the interconnection of the major arteries of town; excavators began to predict where a street would "come out." Panel pictures were still very important to the finders, but the accounts exhibited some awareness of the decorative scheme of the wall as a whole, and of the rooms; the overall color of a wall was noticed, so too the ornamental elements introduced in the design, and occasionally even the composition. Excavation technique remained fairly primitive and conservation ineffectual.

With Fiorelli everything changed as both a scientific method and a systematic program of thorough excavation established a new, objective standard for Pompeian archaeology. Fiorelli had worked on the Pompeian excavations as an archaeologist and numismatist from 1848–1860 but was hampered in the institution of new methods by the entrenched conservatism of the Bourbon administration. When, however, the Kingdom of Naples became part of the united Kingdom of Italy, Fiorelli was immediately put in control of the excavations and given extensive financial support by the national government; within three weeks of his appointment 512 men were at work on the site. During the first year of his directorship, Fiorelli established the *Giornale degli scavi di Pompei* which provided a detailed diary of *each day's* excavations and recorded *everything*, not just the discovery of precious objects or works of art; by this means the raw results of the excavations were made available to the world of classical scholarship.

Fiorelli's regime of fifteen years further established a number of archaeological principles, basic to the understanding of all future work at Pompeii and instrumental in the formation of a scientific technique of excavation to be used by other investigators at other sites. They are:

I.   The creation of a day-book, or meticulously detailed record of everything seen, found, or experienced during the dig as a basis for further analysis and research and as a fundamental record of the site whose history, once disturbed by excavation, cannot otherwise be legitimately recovered.

II. The site of Pompeii was opened to all scholars for their study and potential contribution; a "Scuola di Pompei" was founded, open to Italians and foreigners, many of whom turned to specialized, thematic studies, such as the wall-paintings or the inscriptions, which in turn both supported and amplified the value of the excavations themselves.

III. A distinction was to be made between the archaeological history of the site and the history of the site. As the archaeologist dug into the earth, he was also moving back through time, and different periods would leave their distinct imprint in the earth, if the archaeologist would only take care to notice. Thus, stratigraphy was initiated on the general, if somewhat risky principle that what is lower is older.

IV. In order to control the location of structures and their contents and to place forever all finds in some objective, recoverable, and non-idiosyncratic system, accessible to all subsequent researchers, Fiorelli established a lateral index of map coordinates, divided according to region-block-entry. By this system, which still obtains at Pompeii—although some of the entry numbers have been changed, everything could be located horizontally on the map and was no longer subjected to the vagaries of names. The vertical location of things was more difficult and less systematically defined, relying on the record of the day-book.

V. The excavation of single houses or buildings in isolation was rejected in favor of the programmatic uncovering of entire areas or blocks at one time, beginning at the ground surface and proceeding downwards stratum by stratum. Not only was control of information made easier but the risk of loss in the interstices between excavated areas reduced. Furthermore, the earlier practice with its reliance on narrow trenches led to the destruction of the upper stories which fell down into the undermining trenches. By virtue of the new technique of excavation, the upper parts of a building were preserved and reinforced before continuing down to the next level. Reconstruction of multistoried houses and larger houses, as well as the preservation of overhanging balconies now became possible; architectural reconstructions on the drawing board were less subjected to guesswork, and the history of Roman architecture advanced in accuracy and authority.

VI. Context became more important than contents and isolated finds, even if they were precious. Thus, wherever possible, paintings were left in place and no longer removed as art objects to the Museum in Naples, and the character of the original decorative system was preserved.

Many of these principles, first employed in practice, were enunciated by Fiorelli in his book, *Gli Scavi di Pompei, 1861–1872* (Naples, 1873) which published the results from a decade of excavation right after the fact and attempted to draw coherent conclusions from the evidence presented. Therein he articulated his regionary catalogue and made clear his aim to clear out the unexcavated areas between excavated monuments, such as the zone between the Temple of Isis and the Stabian Baths. Fiorelli also drew the reader's attention to the history of Pompeii as a city, recognizing the significance of levels and the importance of different building techniques as historical markers. Historical topography became possible, since it was clear that the form of Pompeii had not always been fixed in the shape it finally assumed in A.D. 79, and Fiorelli began to speculate on the growth of the town from its primitive origins through

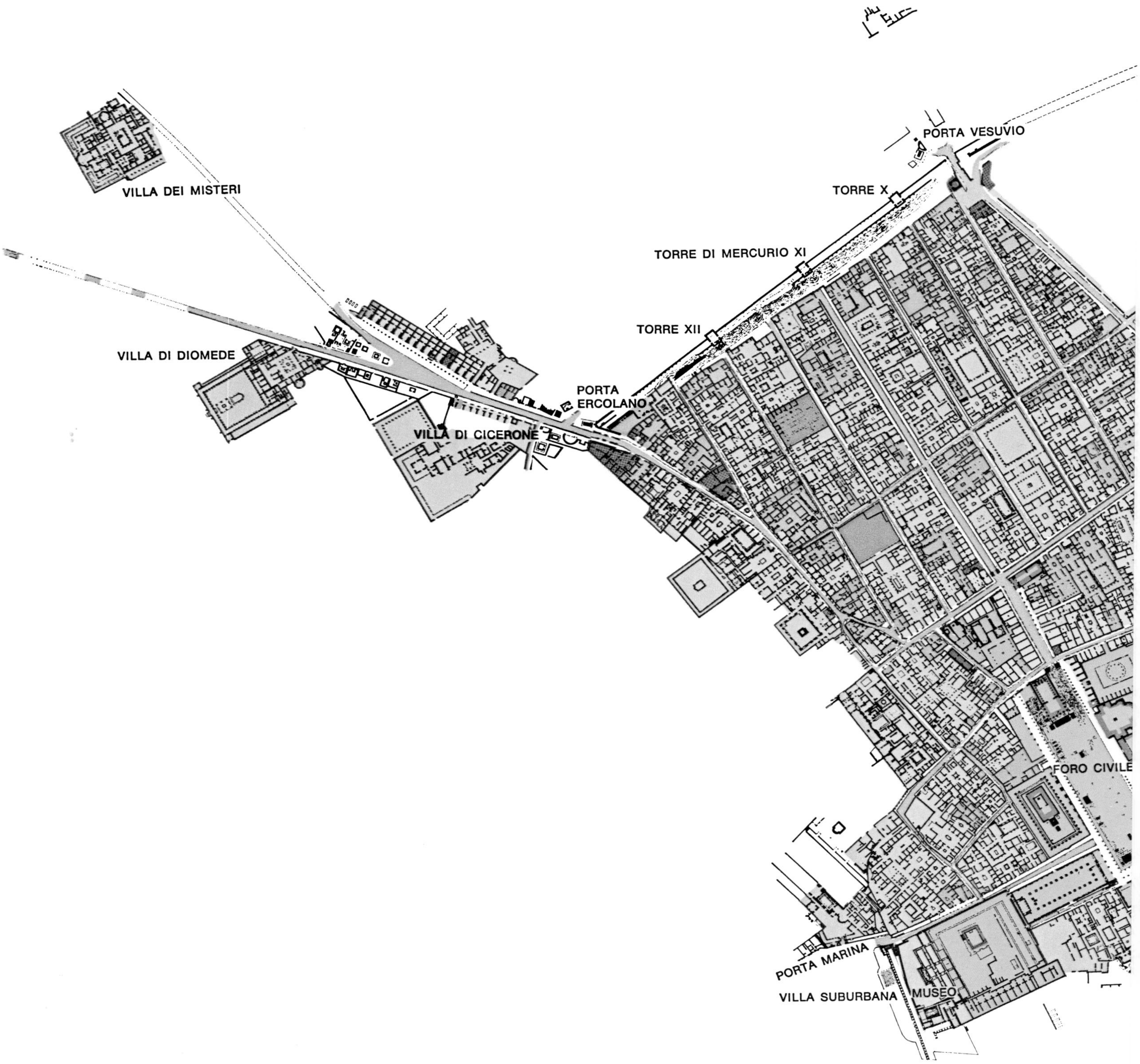

VILLA DEI MISTERI

PORTA VESUVIO

TORRE X

TORRE DI MERCURIO XI

VILLA DI DIOMEDE

TORRE XII

PORTA ERCOLANO

VILLA DI CICERONE

FORO CIVILE

PORTA MARINA

VILLA SUBURBANA   MUSEO

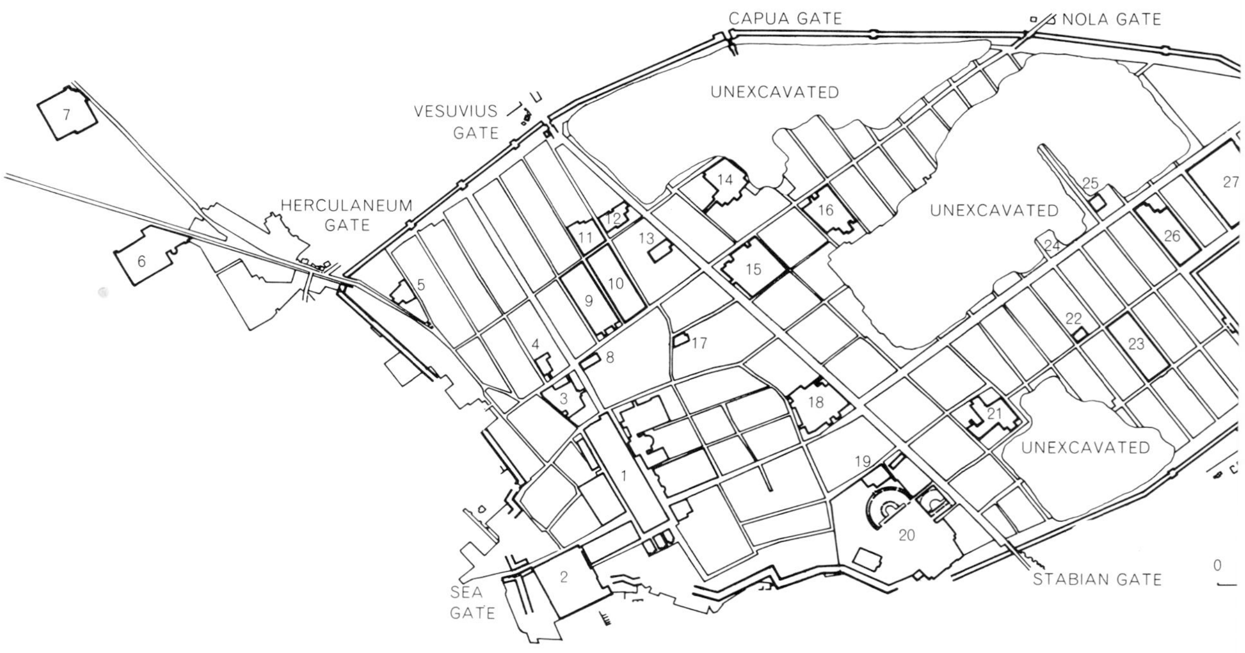

126

CAPUA GATE   NOLA GATE

VESUVIUS GATE

UNEXCAVATED

7

HERCULANEUM GATE

14

25   27

16   UNEXCAVATED

6

12
13   24   26

5   15

9   10   22

4   23

8   17

3   18

21   UNEXCAVATED

1

19

20

SEA GATE   2   STABIAN GATE

0

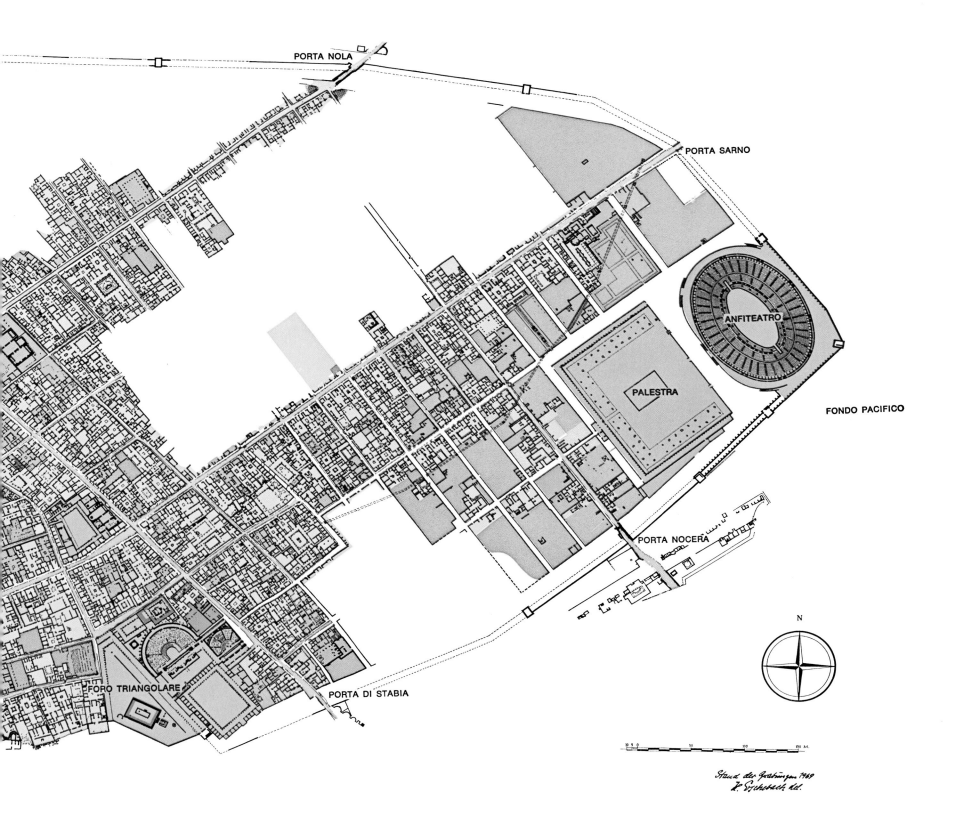

1. Forum
2. Temple of Venus
3. Forum Baths
4. House of the Tragic Poet
5. House of Sallust
6. Villa of Diomedes
7. Villa of the Mysteries
8. Temple of Fortuna Augusta
9. House of the Faun
10. Insula VI, 13
11. House of the Vettii
12. House of the Golden Cupids
13. Fullery
14. House of the Silver Wedding
15. Central Baths
16. House of the Centenary
17. Bakery of Modestus
18. Stabian Baths
19. Temple of Isis
20. Theaters
21. House of Menander
22. Caupona of Euxinus
23. House of the Ship Europa
24. House of Julius Polybius
25. House of Pinarius Cerialis
26. House of Loreius Tiburtinus
27. Praedia of Julia Felix
28. Palaestra

127

Death throes of a watchdog, plaster cast from the impression made when volcanic debris hardened around the corpse. Chained to a stake in the atri of the House of Vesonius Primus and forgotten by his master in the genere panic, the miserable beast tried frantically to get free before finally succumb to suffocation.

a Samnite phase to its rapid development after 80 B.C. when Roman veterans settled there. The new director was also very practical, recognizing that Pompeii was no longer the preserve of the specialist or of the aristocracy but was of growing interest to the educated middle class: he opened a new entrance to the excavations at the Porta Marina near the railroad station and charged admission.

1860

On December 20, Fiorelli appointed director by King Victor Emmanuel.

1861

Excavations began anew with 512 workers in regions VII and VIII; the *Giornale degli Scavi di Pompei* began publication. Foundation of the *Antiquarium* beside the Porta Marina.

1862

Work continued in the zone between the Theater and the Stabian Baths, the *House of Siricus* (VII-1-47) and the *House of the Hanging Balcony* (VII-12-28).

1863

Porta Marina cleared and work continued in the *insulae* (blocks) between the *Strada dell'Abbondanza* and the *Strada degli Augustali* (VII-14, 11, and 12), especially at the corner of the *Strada dei Scheletri* (Skeleton Street) and the *Strada del Lupanare* (Brothel Street)— whether a moral is to be drawn from this connection . . .

Fiorelli or one of his assistants hit upon the idea of pouring plaster into the hollows left by human and animal bodies after they decomposed in the tufa, formed by the hardened, congregated lapilli. Their organic forms could thus be completely recovered, although clothing could be less readily traced.

1865

W. Helbig in *Bollettino dell'Istituto di Corrispondenza Archeologica* 1865, pp. 234–235, mentions the accidental find of two cippi of late antique style, discovered in a layer of sand above the lapilli, giving evidence of the occupation of the site after 79; this observation marked a growing appreciation of the significance of stratification in archaeological research.

General Sherman and a grand company of Americans visited Pompeii and a special excavation in the atrium of VII-7-5 was undertaken with the usual results.

Bacchus, Vesuvius and se
a wall painting found in
the lararium of the House
Centenary. Bacchus is re
in strange attire, wearing
long green tunic covered
bunches of black grapes. I
a thyrsus in one hand wl
out wine for a panther at
with the other. In the bac
is a high mountain wood
parasol pines except at th
at the foot of the mountai
trellises propped by stake
vines are trained. Probab
to portray Vesuvius, this
is the only reliable autho
now known that indicate
of the volcano prior to A
The veneration of Bacchi
might also lead to the ass
that the owner of the hou
the proprietor of a large
Serpents slithered in prof
on countless Pompeian u
were highly touted purve
protection and good luck

130

1869

King Victor Emmanuel visited Pompeii.

1871

Work was concentrated on the eastern part of town, to the east of Strada Stabiana; also work on IX-2 and IX-3 begun. Region-insula numbers now used in the reports.

1872

Porta Stabiana, the area between the Porta Marina and the Temple of Venus, as well as the insula to the south of the Via Marina were all worked on, in some cases returning to excavations begun in 1846–47 and abandoned.

1873

Helbig's *Bollettino* articles concentrated heavily on Pompeian paintings and the organization of the wall.

1875

Fiorelli published his *Descrizione di Pompei* (Naples, 1875) and left for Rome to assume the general direction of museums and excavations in Italy for the national government.

1875

Discovery of a cache of wood-encased, wax writing tablets in the *House of Lucius Caecilius Jucundus*, the Banker (V-1-26).

Michele Ruggiero became director of the excavations (until 1893); he began modern methods of restoration.

1876

The *Giornale degli Scavi di Pompei* ceased to appear; current reports on the excavations were transferred to the *Notizie degli Scavi di Antichità*, published by the Accademia Nazionale dei Lincei in Rome and including archaeological activity in all of Italy.

1877–80

Systematic excavation of *insulae* in Region IX-4, 5, 6 and 7, Region V-1 (extended to 2, 3, and 4 in 1881–1887).

1879

Excavation of the *House of the Centenary* (IX-8-3), named in honor of the eighteenth centennial anniversary of the destruction of Pompeii. The event was marked by official ceremonies and several addresses, including that of Ruggiero wherein he articulated the new policy of restoration and conservation, developed in order to maintain or re-

Gold pendant amulet found in Herculaneum. The nude baby—his hair arranged in ringlet clusters over his ears—is in the act of pouring and could represent either a Lar, the little household god, or a cup bearer.

132

*Bronze phallic lamp, in the Antiquarium,
Pompeii. Both the phallus, as a symbol of
fertility, and bells were used throughout the
Roman Empire as a means of protection
against evil forces—and what could be better
than using both?*

establish the ancient environment as much as possible. This policy is still in effect.

In the German archaeological reports on Pompeii which began with Fiorelli's administration, the articles emphasized the total description of the houses excavated with particular attention given to the plan, overall painted decoration, mosaics, graffiti, and inscriptions. From 1868 on, houses were discussed in order along a street or around an *insula*, complementing the programmatic nature of the new excavation policy; by 1871 the topography of an *insula* (IX-2) was treated entire. These accounts in the *Bollettino dell'Istituto*, written by various German scholars (especially W. Helbig), tended to ignore

133

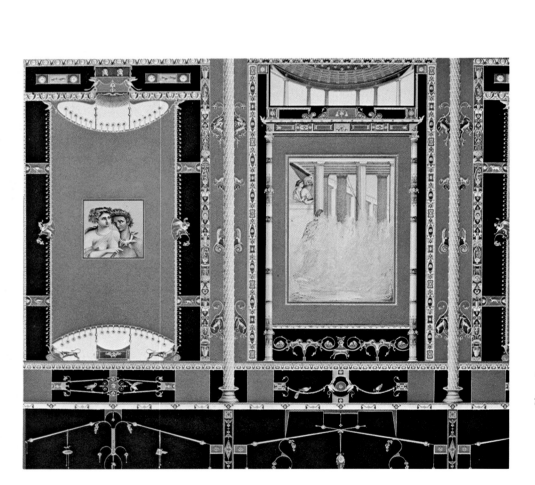

Two 1882 artistic interpretations by Augı *wall decor in the Villa of the Papyri.*

finds, the former center of interest, with the expectation that they would be treated elsewhere, including the *Bollettino Archeologico Napoletano*. However, the importance of finds of a non-artistic character was slowly gaining attention; everyday utensils, industrial objects of various kinds, games, amulets, lamps, tools, etc. merited study because they furnished valuable keys to the understanding of the texture of daily life in all its mundane richness.

Despite Mau's influence, as late as 1869 paintings were still being removed from the walls and transported to the Museum in Naples. Yet before they left the site, the paintings were examined in the context of the total decorative scheme of the wall or of the room, if well enough preserved, and so too were the floor mosaics. By this reordering of priorities scholars came to deal more directly with the character of the whole, whether a room, a house, an *insula*, or the town itself. This approach made possible the development of synthetic studies, not tied to the archaeological history of the site but rather related to general problems or topics brought to light in the course of the excavations. Scholarship, thus, began to focus on classification, thematic analysis, and historical interpretation rather than on the recovery of ruins.

Again, Fiorelli's investigations were instrumental in stimulating this change. His 1873 publication directly faced the problem of the history of Pompeian architecture, the evolution of the city plan, and the development of building techniques. Richard Schöne and Heinrich Nissen studied the same issues in the 1860's and 1870's and published the results in Nissen's *Pompejanische Studien zur Städtekunde des Altertums* (Leipzig, 1877). A somewhat more old-fashioned inventory, but still synthetic in its scope, was J. A. Overbeck's *Pompeji in seinen Gebäuden, Alterthümern und Kunstwerken*, published in several editions (Leipzig, 1856, 1866, 1875), the last with August Mau (1884). Wolfgang Helbig had turned his attention to the comprehensive study of the wall-paintings from the Campanian sites in 1868, largely in catalogue form, but by 1873 in his *Untersuchungen über die campanische Wandmalerei* (Leipzig) he concentrated more heavily on issues of composition.

The master of this line of investigation was August Mau who looked most attentively at the decorative schemes of the wall-paintings rather than at the individual panels. He first published his systematic analysis of these schemes in the *Giornale degli scavi di Pompei* in 1873, and continued to refine and develop his views in articles which

*First Style—the tablinum in the
House of Sallust.*

*Second Style—the Corinthia
House of the Labyrinth.*

136

Fourth Style—the atrium in the House of the Vettii.

Third Style—the large oecus in the Villa Imperiale.

137

appeared almost every year from 1875 to 1898, first in the *Bollettino dell'Istituto* and later in the successor journal, the *Römische Mitteilungen* of the German Archaeological Institute. Supported by the growing body of knowledge about the history of building at Pompeii and by his own increasing sensitivity to changes in the fashion of decorating the walls of Pompeian houses, Mau published his *Geschichte der dekorativen Wandmalerei in Pompeji* (Berlin, 1882), a history of the decorative schemes visible in the paintings themselves when viewed as part of an overall scheme of interior decoration. He called these schemes "Styles" and divided them into historical/typological categories: the *First or Incrusted Style* in the second century B.C. imitated a variety of colored marbles in painted plaster or stucco; the *Second or Architectural Style*, current in the first century B.C., developed illusions of "real" architecture by various means, including perspective; the *Third or Ornamental Style* was developed in Augustan times and re-emphasized the surface, now shaped by delicate, often irrational, ornamentation; and the *Fourth Style* of the first century A.D. which turned the architectural schemes of the Second Style toward fantasy and was robust, often coarse, in its color and composition. Mau thought these schemes succeeded each other neatly in time, but it now appears that the divisions are not so clearly established in history, especially because the evidence of painting in Rome and other major sites indicates a considerable degree of overlap and contamination of Styles. Pompeii, after all, was a conservative, small provincial town, often lagging behind the tastes of the capital. Yet, Mau brought order out of chaos, established the study of Roman wall-painting, and showed that panel pictures, however important, had to be seen in their original context.

Other scholars found other material at Pompeii to excite their interest. The great Roman historian, Theodor Mommsen, visited Pompeii in 1846 where he collected a sack full of graffiti and inscriptions for study. Some of these were published in the *Bollettino*, and by 1852 he presented his *Inscriptiones regni Neapolitani latinae*. R. Garrucci followed with his study of the *Graffiti de Pompei* (Paris, 1856), and later R. Schöne published his authoritative volume in the *Corpus Inscriptionum Latinarum. IV. Inscriptiones parietariae Pompejanae, Herculanenses, Stabianae* (1871), and the world of Roman epigraphy had a treasure trove of rich historical material for study. Other bodies of material, found at Pompeii, were also being collected and published for general purposes of research in Classical Antiquity that transcended the limits of Pompeian studies. Such was H. von

Admiror, O paries, te non cedidisse ruinis qui tot scriptorum taedia sustineas. *(I am surprised, O wall, that you have not fallen down under the burden of so many tedious writers.)*

Gladiatorial graffiti compiled by Niccolini.

Restoration of the Temple of Fortune, an engraving from a drawing by Sir William Gell. Gell undertook this reconstructed version of the temple and triumphal arch in order "to give an idea of the original features of the place, now so disfigured as to be unintelligible. . . ." First using his camera lucida to "draw" the actual appearance of the site, he then restored the ancient aspect of the objects replete with an equestrian statue atop the arch and then added praying Pompeians to lend animation to the scene.

Rohden's publication of *Die Terrakotten von Pompeji* (Stuttgart, 1880), which like the corpus of inscriptions, brought Pompeii itself into the general context of Antiquity. These monographs or catalogues reached a much wider audience than Pompeii enthusiasts, but there were many of those who were served by a different kind of publication.

Gell's *Pompeiana* addressed such an audience, perhaps even more than it met the needs of the scientific community despite the accuracy of the observations and the currency of his account of the excavations. His two-volume edition of 1832 combined many features of interest both to the actual or potential visitor to Pompeii and to the amateur far away from Campania whose knowlege of the ancient places was gathered from reading alone and for his own personal delight. Gell provided a guide-book to the new excavations (since 1819), replete with careful descriptions, plans, line-cuts of many

House of the Tragic Poet . . . before, an engraving from a drawing by Sir William Gell made shortly after its discovery. The drapery had been placed to protect the painting of Achilles from sun damage and the walls faced with tile to preserve them from weather deterioration, giving the effect that the water from the roof fell into the tablinum of the house. Gell "remedied" this impression in his . . .

House of the Tragic Poet . . . after restoration, an engraving from a drawing by Sir William Gell. Drawing the original dimensions with a pane of glass, Gell has added a ceiling, lavish ornamentation and people to produce a pleasing interpretation of how he felt the house must have looked when it served as a residential dwelling.

of the more handsome paintings, and commentaries. But *Pompeiana* also offered a large number of engraved plates with extensive views of the ruins, often peopled by men and women in contemporary dress some of whom are shown in the act of drawing the ancient buildings themselves. Such views were unnecessary for the visitor, but brought Pompeii to the reader. Furthermore, Gell provided a number of reconstructions, some in colored plates, which convey the visual effect of a painted wall or of a mosaic, and others which restore the "original" appearance of rooms or of entire buildings, such as the Temple of Fortune, set in its own square, filled with ancient Pompeians at prayer. Even more effective was Gell's deliberate juxtaposition of *then* and *now* as in his reconstruction of the interior of the *House of the Tragic Poet* which directly follows a view of the same as it is. His justification for doing so is clearly stated:

Poet's House Restored

This restoration is calculated to afford an idea of the pleasing effect which even a moderately-sized house, arranged in the manner of the ancients, is capable of producing. Nothing has been changed from the original drawing . . . , the lines having been traced from it by means of a pane of glass. The roof only has been added, which must have existed, and, probably, in a much more complicated and ornamented form than here represented. The pendent ornaments are taken from a picture at Herculaneum. The light has also been thrown from the contrary side, which has contributed to the apparent change of the picture; and the sombre shades, contrasted with the partial lights of the impluvium and the peristyle, produce an effect scarcely credible by those who have only seen the habitation exposed to the glare of sunshine.[2]

Not only is there an implication that the reconstruction is better than the normal experience of the ruin, but Gell makes no mention of his extensive restoration of the interior decoration nor of the Pompeians who give life to the scene. This desire to recreate ancient Pompeii would have great influence on archaeologists, artists, architects, and authors in the nineteenth century (see following). It also responded to the growing popularity of Pompeii among the general public, witness Robert Burford: *Description of a View of the Ruins of the City of Pompeii, representing the Forum, with adjoining edifices and surrounding country, now exhibiting in the Panorama, Strand; painted from drawings taken on the spot* (London, 1826). So too does George Clarke's two-volume work, *Pompeii* (London, 1832, 1833) in the *Library of Entertaining Knowledge*, issued by the Society for the Diffusion of Useful Knowledge as a companion to the *Library of Useful Knowledge*. The entertainment value of Pompeii would soon be capitalized upon by Bulwer-Lytton in his spectacularly successful novel, *The Last Days of Pompeii* (1834), and by a host of followers.

Great folio volumes, sumptuously illustrated, assisted in the spread of knowledge about Pompeii and in the development of a keen imagery of its once and actual state. C. F. Mazois' *Les Ruines de Pompéi* (4 volumes, Paris, 1824–1838) is a classic of this genre. The work is filled with learned commentary on Pompeian architecture, not restricted to houses, supported by well-executed plans and elevations, and crowned by numerous plates throughout, although color plates begin only with volume III (1829). These volumes enjoyed a wide and influential readership, largely due to the quality of the plates and the accuracy of the architectural renderings, made by Mazois, himself a well-trained architect with many years experience at Pompeii. Nevertheless, the modern reader of Mazois is somewhat disquieted by his statement on p. 21 of the preface to volume I (1824) that the monuments of Pompeii belong to Greek architecture, echoes of the controversy between the "Greeks" and the "Romans" not yet stilled. In the same preface (p.7) Mazois clearly recognizes the significance of Pompeii: "Famous because of its

*A Charles François Mazois reconstr
the decor in the Temple of Jupiter (pa
1829).*

Re-creative presentation of the Temple of Venus (1838, by Charles François Mazois).

destruction alone and never previously the site of important historical events, Pompeii deserves the closest attention as a reservoir of antiquity, not otherwise available, valuable for the study of the past and for the instruction of the present." These sentiments eventually found their way into a less impressive work by W. H. Davenport Adams, *The Buried Cities of Campania; or Pompeii and Herculaneum* (London, 1868); he states in his preface (p. v): "But this third-rate provincial town—the 'Brighton' or 'Scarborough' of the Roman patricians, though less splendid and far less populous than the English watering places—owes its celebrity to its very destruction."

If the somber emphasis on the terrible destruction of Pompeii was to become a leitmotiv of romanticism, the glorification of the ancient town still had its bright moments. In 1854 Fausto Niccolini began the publication of his magnificent *Le Case ed i monumenti di Pompei* (4 volumes, Naples, 1854–1896, 418 plates), itself a monument to quality book production in the nineteenth century, a skillful achievement of careful description coupled with vivid, highly imaginative reconstruction. Volume I (1854) thoroughly treats many of the famous houses and buildings including the Houses of the Tragic Poet, of Castor and Pollux, of the Faun, of Marcus Lucretius, the Temples of Isis and of Fortuna, the Stabian Baths, and many others. Volume II (1863) concentrates on the Villa of Diomedes and on the general description of the town; volume III (1890) returns to the more varied format of the first volume with several houses being discussed—the Houses of L. Caecilius Jucundus, of the Centenary, of Sallust—but the greater attention is given to essays on topography, on trade and industry in Pompeii, and on Pompeian art, lavishly illustrated, and on the plaster recreations of the bodies of the dead. Volume IV (1896) is justly famous for its stimulating "Saggi del restauro," Niccolini's vivid, watercolor reconstructions of the public areas, streets, shops, and busy places of ancient Pompeii. These volumes mix the old and new concepts of Pompeian archaeology, and they were never equalled in range of treatment nor in quality of illustration. If Niccolini's inspired reconstructions shaped the imagery of recreated Pompeii for decades, they also responded to the physical reconstitution of Pompeian architecture, variously attempted in nineteenth-century Europe.

Reconstructions of two wall paintings found in the peristyle of the House of the Physician. The top picture shows pygmies attacking a hippopotamus and capturing a crocodile in a Nile landscape; the bottom painting, entitled "The Judgment of Solomon," portrays the Biblical characters as pygmies (by Niccolini).

House of the Faun from the street entrance with visitors inside the peristyle garden (by Niccolini).

Wall painting of wild beasts, found on the garden wall in the House of the Epigrams; a leopard attacks a bull while a Silenus lays sprawled out with his silver drinking cup below (a Niccolini reconstruction).

Reconstruction of a wall in a Pompeian house by Niccolini.

Wall decor of a Pompeian house (a Niccolini reconstruction).

*Scene beside the Mercury Fountain with thermopolium in the background
(a Niccolini reconstruction).*

View of the Temple of Jupiter and the Forum (a Niccolini reconstruction).

Decor detail of the baths beside the Stabian Gate (a Niccolini reconstruction).

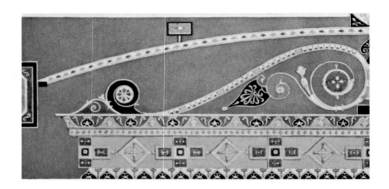

The lush opulence of the Villa of Diomedes is captured in these two 1825 decorative interpretations by John Goldicutt. The fragment detail of the wall decor with its rich highlights is enlarged in the side of an apartment in typical Pompeian red and black.

As it had done in the eighteenth century, Pompeii continued to influence the design of costume, objets de toilette, house and personal furnishings, furniture, and interior decoration, often with increasing archaeological correctness at the price of less delicacy and spontaneity. John Goldicutt's book, *Specimens of Ancient Decorations from Pompeii* (London, 1825), typified this development, since the work was designed to assist the artist in the interior decoration of houses by providing ancient models eminently

154

Leda, beloved wife of the King of Sparta, also caught the eye of Zeus who came to her in the shape of a swan, and by enfolding her in his wings fathered two of her children (according to Greek mythology). Pictured here are the original wall painting of Leda and her lover in feathery form from Stabiae and Wilhelm Zahn's watercolor counterpart.

suitable for the purpose. The painter, Wilhelm Zahn, friend of Goethe and familiar at Pompeii, compiled his *Die schönsten Ornamente und merkwürdigsten Gemälde aus Pompeji, Herculaneum und Stabiae* (Berlin, 1827–1859) in the form of a hodge-podge of plans, line-drawings of works of art, colored reconstructions of painted walls and mosaics, and bands of ornament, not merely to record them but to affect the course of contemporary art—Winckelmann, as it were, in a minor key. This approach was particularly congenial to that development of garden and landscape imagery in romantic Germany which

Diana, twin sister of Apollo, was a great favorite in Roman religion and endowed with multi-mythological powers—as a huntress as shown here with bow and arrow, as the goddess of marriage and childbirth, and perhaps uppermost as the deity of the moon. The wall painting below was found at Stabiae, and we are indebted to Wilhelm Zahn for the watercolor reconstruction to the left.

156

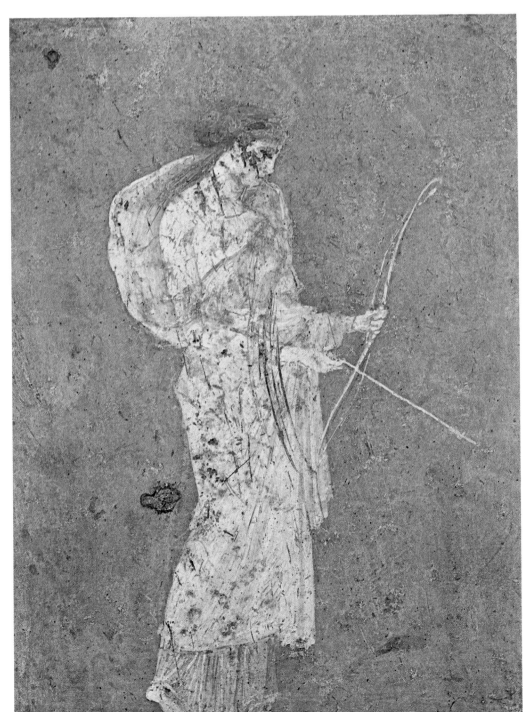

Primavera was the personification of Spring, pictured here trailing flowers as she heralds the arrival of that season. Stabiae was the source of the original wall painting; Wilhelm Zahn supplied the modern painted interpretation.

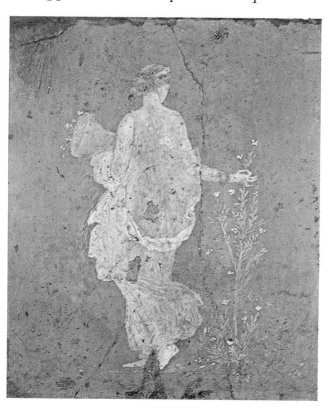

Gods and goddesses galore grace the paintings found on the walls of Pompeii, and among the most popular subjects were the star-crossed lovers, Perseus and Andromeda. Found chained to a rock in danger of having her toes nibbled away by a sea monster, Andromeda was rescued by Perseus, but only after a series of vicissitudes that would have overcome mere mortals did they manage to live happily ever after in mythology-land. This 1833 Zahn painting of the Eros-blessed couple is a rendering of an original wall-painting found in the House of the Colored Capitals.

Jupiter was honored as the supreme deity in the Roman ruling trinity. In Greece known as Zeus—and sometimes called Jove by the Romans— Jupiter sits at his ease in this picture but with his requisite thunderbolt sceptre at the ready should its use become necessary. The original painting upon which this Wilhelm Zahn representation of 1828 was based was found on the wall of the portico in the House of Castor and Pollux (the Dioscuri and, incidentally, the twin sons of Leda) where, because of exposure to the elements, it was ruined beyond recognition.

Interior of the Pompejanum, a Pompeian-style villa at Aschaffenburg
designed by Friedrich von Gärtner for Ludwig I of Bavaria.

opened to the mind's eye the fecund world of the interior. It was not, however, restricted
to Germany—witness the Pompeian Room in the Garden Pavilion at Buckingham
Palace and the Pompeian Court in London's Crystal Palace (1851).

More substantial, certainly, was the reproduction of a Pompeian villa built for
Ludwig I of Bavaria as a country refuge. The Pompejanum at Aschaffenburg was
designed by Friedrich von Gärtner around 1839–1840 for his royal and self-indulgent
patron, who had himself visited Pompeii in 1829. Gärtner loosely but effectively based
his design on the Houses of the Questor and of the Dioscuri (Castor and Pollux),
creating an open pavilion of distinguished character whose decoration depended heavily
on published reconstructions of Pompeian walls. Like so many of its models,
unfortunately, the Pompejanum is now in ruins, but its modern counterpart, the J. Paul
Getty Museum in Malibu, California, lives.

The Pompeian Room in the Garden Pavilion located in the gardens at Buckingham Palace, designed by Agosino Aglio and built in 1844 by L. Grüner at the instigation of the Prince Consort. As the years took their toll, the Pavilion became shabby and run-down and was subsequently demolished in 1928.

*The mosaic fountain pictured, from the predominantly Pompeian J. Paul Getty
Museum in Malibu, California, is a virtual facsimile of the fountain for which the House of
the Great Fountain was named—probably Pompeii's most sumptuous. Flanked by two
marble theater masks and completely faced in fabulous mosaics with a mask of Oceanus
worked into the motif, the water trickles down through the narrow slit in the center of the niche
running down the steps into the basin.*

Perhaps the most spectacular of these attempts to recapture the past through architecture was the Maison Pompéienne, built for Prince Jérome Napoléon ("Plonplon") on the Avenue Montaigne in Paris. Originally entrusted to the architect, Auguste Rougevin, he died en route to Pompeii to select appropriate models. In 1856 a younger architect, Alfred-Nicolas Normand, was entrusted with the commission which he completed in 1860. Normand knew Pompeii and Pompeian architecture at first hand, and indeed had drafted an elaborate reconstruction of the House of the Faun as one of his projects while at the French School in Rome. Yet, he seems to have incorporated elements in his design that were only partly derived from his personal experience and relied heavily on the plates in Gell and Mazois as well as on other reconstructions. The result fell somewhere between Pompeii and Second Empire with a possible touch of Sir John Soane's house in London thrown in, especially in the dramatic atrium of the Maison. Prince Napoléon filled the house with miscellaneous antiquities, including objects from Pompeii, Greek bronzes, inscriptions, Imperial eagles, Napoleonic masks, and contemporary paintings. For political reasons the Prince soon left his residence, it passed from hand to hand, and was pulled down in 1891.

The writer Théophile Gautier (*Le Palais Pompéien. Etudes sur la maison gréco-romaine*, Paris, 1866) stated that the Maison was based on the House of the Tragic Poet, on the House of Pansa, and especially on the Villa of Diomedes, one of the best known of all Pompeian houses at the time because of its large rooms, fine garden, and many corpses. Gautier had used the Villa as the site of his Pompeian novella, *Arria Marcella* (also known as *Pompeia*), first published in 1852 and by 1863 included among his *Romans et Contes*. He had included an extensive, if sycophantic, description of the Villa of Diomedes in the novella which was closer in many respects to the Maison than to Pompeii. Similarly, the academic painter, Gustave Boulanger, showed his painting, *The Rehearsal of "The Flute Player" in the Atrium of the House of H.I.H. Prince Napoléon*, at the Salon of 1861 and attempted to combine two modes of aesthetic distinction. The painting represented a soirée in the atrium of the Maison with Gautier, the French poet and dramatist, Emile Augier—whose work was being recited—and Prince Jérome, present and in antique costume, as if the intellectual life of a rich, educated Pompeian household had returned to its natural arena, but in Paris. Still, Boulanger's painting did

The Atrium of the Maison Pompéienne, built for Prince Jérome Napoléon ("Plonplon"), an oil painting by Gustave Boulanger, from the Chateau Museum at Versailles.

not quite bring the past back to life, and neither did the Dutch-English artist Lawrence Alma-Tadema, the "Painter of the Victorian Vision of the Ancient World" who incorporated several Pompeian settings into his work, and with even greater attentiveness to archaeological detail.

Alfred-Nicolas Normand has another Pompeian connection. In September 1851, he took 55 photographic views of buildings at Pompeii and subsequently printed them in the calotype process. These photographs of the Forum, the Temples of Jupiter, of Fortune, and of Apollo, of the Street of Tombs, of the Amphitheater, of the Herculaneum

164

Sir Lawrence Alma-Tadema measuring ruins and examining marble at Pompeii during his honeymoon visit in 1863.

Alma-Tadema's interest in the Roman world is manifested in this painting of Caracalla being welcomed home (note the Pompeian house in the background).

Gate, of the Houses of the Faun, of Pansa, of Actaeon, and of Castor and Pollux, and of various shops must be among the earliest photographs taken of Pompeii. Only a few years later, Thomas H. Dyer used photographs to illustrate his *The Ruins of Pompeii. Photographic Views with a History of the Destruction of the City* (London, 1866), and was soon followed by others, most notably L. Fischetti, *Pompeii, Past and Present, illustrated by Photographs of the Ruins as they are, with sketches of their original elevations* (London, 1884; french edition, Naples, 1886). And yet photography did not become important in the scientific or touristic world of Pompeii until very late in the nineteenth century, even after inexpensive cameras became available. Perhaps the reason may be found in the nature of the photographic image whose apparent reality did not jibe very well with that imaginary view of the ancient town, so carefully created by scholars and poets. The drama of destruction seemed to demand more than the prose of the photograph.

In 1827 T. L. Donaldson, architect, published his *Pompeii, illustrated with picturesque views, engraved by W. B. Cooke from the original drawings of Lieut. Col. Cockburn of the Royal Artillery, and with plans and details of the public and domestic edifices, including the recent excavations and a descriptive letterpress to each plate* (2 volumes, London). This highly derivative work depended heavily on Mazois and other Pompeianists for its diluted scholarship. Furthermore, despite Cockburn's explicit statement that his "desire is to produce accurate drawings of the state of the ruins rather than fictitious corrections or fanciful reconstructions" (preface, p. 1), the reference to "picturesque views" in the title belies the legitimacy of his statement. Indeed, he follows a tradition that goes back into the eighteenth century and was exploited only a few years earlier by Henry Wilkins in his *Suite de vues pittoresques des ruines de Pompeii* (Rome, 1819). The author strikes another note when he emphasizes that the value of Pompeii lies in the evidence it provides of the private life of the ancients, even at the cost of the "dreadful catastrophe" which destroyed Herculaneum, Stabiae, and Pompeii, "lamentable as it is to contemplate in all its horror and desolation." Although it may be difficult for the reader to judge which gave the greater pleasure, the recovery of Pompeian life or the contemplation of its terrible destruction by Vesuvius, the personalization of the experience which transcends the limitations of time is a hallmark of romanticism. "Visions of Vesuvius" and ruminations on ruins are romantic themes informing many works of pictorial and literary art in the nineteenth century, not least of all in John Hughes' *Pompeii, A Descriptive Ode* which stands before the text of Donaldson's book:

Stranger, wouldst though yet unfold
A tale of deeper wreck and woe?
Dark are the mysteries that sleep below;
Sad are the legends of the times of old.
Thy foot is on a city's grave:

Mute is the hall of pomp, the social hearth,
Deep whelm'd beneath the burning wave
Far from the cheerful light of upper earth;
And o'er the ominous surface of their tomb
Fond Man renews his toils—to meet a second doom.

Or, meditating on with pensive tread,
Pause; mark yon roofless walls,
Where Echo's self appals,
As in some silent chamber of the dead.
Five hundred years thrice told
Slow o'er their bed have roll'd,
Swept from the busy paths of short-liv'd men,
Ere Fate the spell unseal'd,
Their prison-house reveal'd,
And rais'd reluctant up their buried heads again.

Lo! Time hath check'd his withering arm
O'er all thine eyes around survey;
And, as of those who perish'd yesterday,
Preserves Man's every trace distinct and warm.

· ·

Where now the populous town, the varied soil
Cool'd by fresh shade, or waving thick with corn?
The olive-groves, the vine-clad heights, where Morn
Smil'd once on a wide scene of happy toil?
Lo, as those heavy clouds slow roll'd away,
And left distinct Vesuvius' towering head,
Broad from his summit to the circling bay
A barren plain of whiten'd ashes spread;
A silent waste, uncheer'd by living breath;
—A pale and glittering tomb—a wilderness of death.

Perhaps all those skeletons found at Pompeii spoke too strongly of lives cut down, terribly and suddenly, vivid and stark witnesses of the transiency of life, poignant symbols of the swift destruction of the ancient, once bustling town. Preoccupation with ruination and death exercised multiple effects on the romantic mind contemplating Pompeii. The ruins themselves could be seen as skeletons, no longer a living, complete architecture, and hence cut off from the present. So French architects like Henri Labrouste came to believe around 1830 when reconstructions and adaptations of the ancient monuments were held to be more alive than the broken fragments on which they were based. Thus, the stubborn, long life of the reconstructions, separated from the reality of the ruined buildings, no longer acceptable as valid statements of their pristine condition, even to the archaeologist.

The abundant evidence of death and destruction encouraged a pathetic indulgence in sentiment that delighted in contrast: the happy beauty of Pompeii before A.D. 79 transformed so quickly by terror and destruction into desolation; the unknown buried ruins, hidden from men, emerging with the archaeologists' spade to a glorious state which may once again inspire men. Such are the sentiments of Thomas Babington Macaulay's poem *Pompeii* which won the Chancellor's medal at the Cambridge commencement in July, 1819:

> Go, seek Pompeii now:—with pensive tread
> Roam through the silent city of the dead . . .
> And muse in silence on a people's grave.
>
> . . . .
>
> And thou, sad city, raise thy drooping head,
> And share the honours of the glorious dead . . .
> Now shall thy deathless mem'ry live entwin'd
> With all that conquers, rules or charms the mind, . . .
> Thy fame shall snatch from time a greener bloom, . . .

The line "Pompeii, the city of the dead" runs like some melancholic refrain in those nineteenth-century minds gifted with a strong historical imagination. So apparently Sir Walter Scott repeatedly exclaimed when he visited Pompeii in the company of Sir William Gell on February 9, 1832. A colorful account of this visit was inserted into a lecture delivered at the City Hall, Burlington, on December 4, 1855 by one James W. Wall:

Several years ago, there trod the lonely streets of Pompeii, with feeble step and slow, a grey haired man. Physical suffering, and mental toil, had passed their ploughshares over that noble brow, with a subsoil pressure. The mind within, which like a lamp in a vase of alabaster had once 'illumed' that fine old face, was burning dimly now, or only flickered up with a sort of supernatural light, as dying lamps will, just before they are extinguished. The powers that had so long delighted the world, recalling past ages and manners with such vividness, that men believed he had found the enchanter's wand of the great wizard of his house, were now all gone. But as that old man paced mournfully through the deserted streets, and by the hearth-stones, cold and cheerless, of the exhumed city, his head drooped upon his noble chest, and he murmured, 'Take me away from this; take me away from this; 'tis the City of the Dead; the City of the Dead'—then wept like a child.[3]

Even the great historian of medieval Rome, Ferdinand Gregorovius, who visited Pompeii on August 23, 1853, wrote in his journal for that day:

The houses stand like empty coffins; rows of streets; temples, theatre, and Forum—all still as death, shimmering under the spell of summer. Never did I experience such melancholy; none but a poet could express it.[4]

A year later Gregorovius returned to Pompeii in the company of Giuseppe Fiorelli who showed him the new excavations, the plaster casts of Pompeian fugitives who did not get away, and once again the Villa of Diomedes. The last awakened memories, because Gregorovius had answered that appeal to express his thoughts in poetry with his poem, *Euphorion*, set largely in the Villa of Diomedes and made historically true by the incorporation of much archaeological material—not necessarily to the advantage of his Muse.

"Savage State or Commencement of Empire," episode 1 of The Course of Empire, *an oil painting by Thomas Cole, 1836, from the Reed Collection, New York Gallery of Fine Arts.*

Skeletons also inspired Thomas Gray to write a novel, *The Vestal, A Tale of Pompeii* (Boston, 1830), which mixed together archaeology and homiletics. Episodes in the novel were tied to various skeletons as keys to Roman life past, since melodrama made moral strictures more palatable; the central characters, Lucius and Lucilla, are converted to Christianity only to sacrifice themselves during the eruption by refusing to leave the heroine's mother behind. This moralizing gloss did tend to deaden things, and it became increasingly difficult to assume Shelley's positive view of Pompeii:

> I stood within the city disinterred;
> And heard the autumnal leaves like light footfalls
> Of spirits passing through the streets; and heard
> The Mountain's slumberous voice at intervals
> Thrill through those roofless halls; . . .
> —*Ode to Naples* (1820)

170

"Destruction," episode 4 of The Course of Empire, *an oil painting by Thomas Cole, 1836, from the Reed Collection, New York Gallery of Fine Arts.*

The tendency to moralize on the destruction of Pompeii proved irresistible, especially when greater attention was given to the people of Pompeii as they became better known through the recovery of the furnishings of their daily lives. The perishability of civiliations and of empires—an old, even pre-Christian theme—was avidly taken up by the romantics, confirmed in their suspicion that nothing lasted by the presence of ruins. Thomas Cole's great series, *The Course of Empire* in the New York Historical Society (completed 1836), offers a visually powerful interpretation of this theme. It is, however, not generally stated but, instead, is focused on the Classical world, stimulated, it would appear, by the reverberations of Pompeii's destruction. William Giles Dix, an American poet and admirer of the romantic painter, Washington Allston, may well have combined Cole's vision and his own knowledge of Pompeii in a long poem, *Pompeii*, which he published in 1848 (Boston):

Thoughtful the silent streets we tread
Of this wide city of the dead,
And gaze on the now quiet scene,
Calling to mind what once hath been,
When not the curious stranger here
Alone was walking, moved with fear
Of God . . .
But when, through each close, crowded street,
Was heard the sound of hurried feet,
As quicker, nearer, hither came
The cloud of ashes, whilst the flame
Of the high, burning, quaking mount,
Bursting from out the fiery fount, . . .
With what dismay and dread alarms,
Close pressed within affection's arms,
Are held the dearest, fondest ones,—
Fathers and mothers, daughters, sons,—
While stifled cries and shortened breath
Proclaim the approach to strangling death
To all, who in this hour of gloom
Await their sad, terrific doom . . .
The columns of the Forum stand,
Where oft full many an earnest band,
Assembling, talked with zeal and might,
Of freedom, victory, glory, right; . . .
About us broken pillars lie,
Whose massive forms, in days gone by,
Supported the majestic fane,
Or stately arch; but now in vain
Their chiselled grandeur meets the sight,
A graceful architecture light
Only the traveller's wonder gains.
How much around us yet retains
Some portion of its ancient grace,
Which years on years cannot efface!

. . . .

When the mysterious hours were past,
In which Pompeii was o'ercast,
How desolate the place and rude
Where had the beauteous city stood!
The noble structures Art had made
Were now full deep in darkness laid . . .

172

The apocalyptic vision of the destruction of Pompeii on August 24, A.D. 79 took precedence as the prime image of the death of the past. Sumner Lincoln Fairfax wrote a nearly endless poem (200 pages), entitled *The Last Night of Pompeii* (New York, 1832), in which he expounded on the moral and social corruption of the people, properly punished by an act of divine retribution, as if Pompeii were some Roman Sodom. The implicit melodrama of the moment of destruction and the awful horror of the event were fully visualized in John Martin's stunning painting, *The Destruction of Pompeii and Herculaneum* in Manchester (after 1821), based on Pliny's *Letters* and Gell's *Pompeiana* and influenced by J. M. W. Turner's cataclysmic skies. Martin specialized in catastrophes and painted large canvases representing *The Deluge*, *The Fall of Babylon*, and *The Destruction of Sodom and Gomorrah*.

A Russian painter, Karl Bryullov, also painted *The Last Days of Pompeii* in 1828 (The Hermitage, Leningrad) and filled it with lightning flashes, the destruction of buildings and statuary, fleeing figures, and much bathos. Although the painting relies heavily on contemporary archaeological reports, it somewhat resembles a Neapolitan presepio; perhaps all these elements contributed to its success in touring Europe. In 1833 Bryullov's painting was exhibited at the Brera in Milan, where six years earlier in 1827 at La Scala an opera had been staged with music by Giovanni Pacini, libretto by A. L. Tottola, entitled *L'Ultimo giorno di Pompei*. Alessandro Sanquirico designed the spectacular sets for the opera and constantly emphasized the brooding, later explosive presence of Vesuvius. This was not the only opera on the subject of Pompeii, as Julius Pabst wrote one similarly entitled *Die letzten Tage von Pompeji*, which was performed in Dresden in 1851.

An earnest young Englishman, Edward Bulwer-Lytton, might have heard of Pacini's opera. He did, however, see Bryullov's *The Last Days of Pompeii* on exhibit in Milan and was much taken with its grand composition and crashing effect. In 1834 he published his archaeological novel, *The Last Days of Pompeii*, written in Naples 1832–33 and dedicated to Sir William Gell. It was a smashing success in the English-speaking world and in Germany and went into several editions, for a time surpassing even Dickens in popularity. Benjamin Disraeli, Thomas Macaulay, Mary Shelley, Harriet Martineau, Charles Kingsley, Robert Browning, Elizabeth Barrett Browning, Charles Dickens, and Charles Reade liked Bulwer-Lytton's book; Thomas Carlyle, Thackeray, and Alfred Lord Tennyson did not. The principal characters of the novel soon became famous—*Glaucus* and *Ione*, the heroic, virtuous lovers; *Nydia*, the beautiful, blind slave-girl; *Julia*, the spoiled daughter of Diomed; and *Arbaces*, the vicious, mysterious priest of Isis—and so too the setting in Pompeii on the eve of its ruination. Glaucus' own house is that of the Tragic Poet, and the lively street scenes are closely dependent on Gell's reconstructions. The great success of the novel is due to many factors: the melodramatic situation which involves both the principal characters and the townspeople in deep danger, the personal conflict between requited and unrequited lovers, the contrast between the voluptuous life of pagan Pompeii and the advent of pious Christians, and inevitably the brooding, tragic awareness of impending doom. Surely, the book owes some of its popularity to Bulwer-Lytton's convincing portrayal of Pompeii as a city of the living, not of the dead. It is that quality which struck Mary Shelley writing in 1843 of her second visit to Pompeii:

Bulwer has peopled its silence. I have been reading his book, and I have felt on visiting the place much as if *really* it had once been full of stirring life, now that he has attributed names and possessors to its houses, passengers to its streets. Such is the power of imagination . . . it can put a soul into stones, and hang the vivid interest of our passions and our hope upon objects otherwise vacant of name or sympathy . . . but the account of its 'Last Days' has cast over it a more familiar garb, and peopled its deserted streets with associations that greatly add to their interest.

The novel also inspired a number of artists to create images either of its climactic episodes, as in James Hamilton's painting, *The Last Days of Pompeii*, 1864 (Brooklyn Museum), or of the major characters, like Randolph Rogers' *Nydia, the Blind Girl of Pompei*, 1856, a marble statue made in more than fifty replicas. Strangely enough, the

Marble statue of Nydia, the blind slave-girl who saved the day for Glaucus and Ione—the virtuous lovers of Bulwer-Lytton's The Last Days of Pompeii—*by leading them to the safety of the sea. Sculpted by Randolph Rogers, 1856, from* The Brooklyn Museum.

174

*Marble relief of theater masks, probably
originally part of a panel in a Pompeian
garden, composed of a standard cast of
characters in a Greek comedy: a conniving
slave (right), a circumspect youth (left) who
seeks the hand of the daughter of the elderly
gentleman (below) and an omnipresent satyr
(behind the young man).*

*Rehearsal of a Satyr Play, a mosaic from the tablinum of the House of the
Tragic Poet. The bearded, sandaled figure with the two masks at his feet is
the chorus master. He is watching two actors in loincloths practice dance
steps to the accompaniment of an aulos player. To the right an attendant is
assisting another actor into costume beside a mask-topped table.*

"The smell of the greasepaint, the roar of the
crowd" a century apart. Niccolini's visitors
contemplated the Great Theater in the 1850's.
Von Matt's twentieth-century version shows all
is still in readiness for Act One to begin.

Two stage sets from the House of Pinarius Cerialis used in home productions.

Street musicians and a comedy scene, two companion mosaic pieces from the Villa of Cicero. The three musicians—a tambourine player, one holding tiny hand cymbals and an aulos player—cavort about the small stage, while a hard-to-please dwarf watches in stony silence. The three women and boy in the comedy scene sit clustered around a small table with serious faces. Both scenes were signed by Dioscurides, a mosaic artist from Samos.

most interesting character of all—the Gothic villain, Arbaces—did not receive his due in the visual arts, although the locus of his unprincipled activity, the Temple of Isis, had long caught the imagination of romantics like William Beckford who fell into a reverie of pagan horrors when he visited the site in 1780.

Interest in Bulwer-Lytton's novel diminished after 1850, but it was still being read decades after publication. N. Scotti wrote *Three Houses in Pompeii; a real and practical guide-book, compiled in harmony with the description given by Bulwer-Lytton in his "Last Days" in 1907* (Naples), and several motion pictures were made of it in the twentieth century with more or less fidelity, with mixed success, and to mixed reviews.

Bulwer-Lytton had launched the Pompeian novel, and, in addition to outright or covert piracies, there were many emulators of the genre. P. Koerber wrote a novel, *Diomedes and Clodius* (Nürnberg, 1850) for children, which hardly departed from its source, and the popular German novelist, Woldemar Kaden, made an industry of Pompeii with his production of novellas, short stories, and journalistic accounts, not all of them located in antiquity. Many of them, in fact, seem to have been intended for the German tourist, bound for Pompeii and prepared to mix fact, fantasy, and good simple pleasure, as the illustrations of his writing in the popular magazines indicate.

Other novelists were moved by more complicated emotions. Théophile Gautier published his novella, *Arria Marcella* (1852), partly under the influence of the imprint of a woman's bosom found in the Villa of Diomedes, filled in with plaster, and then preserved in the Naples Museum. At least his hero, Octavian, was so deeply moved by that bosom that he fell in love with its original, brought back to life by the intensity of his desire. Fortunately for him, he was rescued from this beautiful ghost by Arrius, a Christian ghost, so that he could return to the real world and marry a nice English girl—bosom unspecified.

The German novelist, Wilhelm Jensen, wrote his Pompeian novel, *Gradiva* (1903), featuring a benighted archaeologist, Norbert Hanold, who fell in love with a young woman's foot, first seen on a Roman bas-relief and then assiduously followed to Pompeii. There Hanold too succumbed to the lure of the past, thought he had found the ancient owner of the lovely foot reborn, and was delighted, ultimately, to emerge from his trance to discover that the owner of that foot existed, was walking around in his own world, and could be loved and love him in return. *Gradiva* is not a very good novel, but

182

it did find a very attentive reader, Sigmund Freud, who wrote his classic work, *Der Wahnen und die Träume in W. Jensens 'Gradiva'* (Vienna, 1907, 2nd edition 1912), known in America under the title, *Delusion and Dream. An Interpretation in the Light of Psychoanalysis of Gradiva, a Novel, by Wilhelm Jensen* (translated by Helen M. Downey, New York, 1917).

More than a century before, Beckford had understood the dream-like quality of an experience in Pompeii, the reality of the reveries encouraged by the ruins and all they represented. Gautier himself had recognized effect of the rapid transition from one time to another, forcefully experienced at Pompeii:

The three friends alighted at the Pompeii Station, amused by the mixture of antiquity and modern times naturally suggested to the mind by the title, 'Pompeii Station;' a Greco-Roman city, and a railroad terminus!
Surprising indeed is the aspect of Pompeii. Even the most prosaic and least intelligent natures are amazed by the sudden retrogression of nineteen centuries. In two steps one passes from modern to antique life, from Christianity to Paganism.[5]

Not everyone responded in the same way:

We came out from under the solemn mysteries of this city of the Venerable Past—this city which perished, with all its old ways and its quaint old fashions about it, remote centuries ago, when the Disciples were preaching the new religion, which is as old as the hills to us now—and went dreaming among the trees that grow over acres and acres of its still buried streets and squares, till a shrill whistle and the cry of '*All aboard—last train for Naples!*' woke me up and reminded me that I belonged in the nineteenth century, and was not a dusty mummy, caked with ashes and cinders, eighteen hundred years old. The transition was startling. The idea of a railroad-train actually running to old dead Pompeii, and whistling irreverently, and calling for passengers in the most bustling and businesslike way, was as strange a thing as one could imagine, and as unpoetical and disagreeable as it was strange.[6]

—Mark Twain, *Innocents Abroad*

For those who watched the fireworks display at Manhattan Beach in the summer of 1885, there were no "Last Days of Pompeii," just a spectacular delusion of the night that extinct Pompeii had returned to extinguish itself, once again, for their pleasure.

DESCRIPTIVE
MUSIC

"THE LAST DAYS OF POMPEI

TO BE PRODUCED IN FIREWORKS, SEASON OF 1885, UNDER THE DIRECTION OF J

MANHATTAN BEA

184

Poster advertisement of the Manhattan Beach fireworks display in 1885 purported to be a replica representation of "The Last Days of Pompeii."

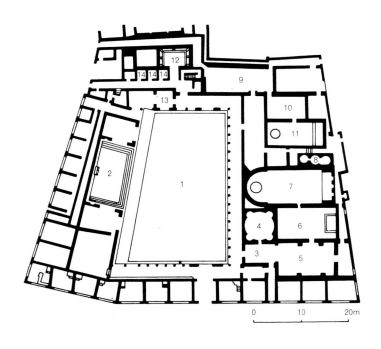

Plan of the Stabian Baths

1. Palaestra
2. Swimming pool (natatio)
3. Entrance hall
4. Cold bath (frigidarium; formerly a laconicum or dry hot-air bath)
5. Dressing room (apodyterium)
6. Warm room (tepidarium)
7. Hot bath (caldarium)
8. Furnaces
9. Women's apodyterium
10. Women's tepidarium
11. Women's caldarium
12. Latrine
13. Bath supervisor's office
14. Individual "hip bath" cubicles

The baths (thermae) of Pompeii can be compared to a present-day combination club/ cum café/cum health spa with, sometimes, a gymnasium thrown in. Here, in a single establishment, the local citizenry could receive physical care, enjoy creature comforts, carry on a bit of business, do a little politicking, gossip with their friends and the bath attendants, dine or sip a libation, and generally spend a convivial couple of hours in relaxing rejuvenation. The prescribed form of the bath followed an established pattern. First there was a court (palaestra) surrounded by a colonnade, used for exercise—gymnastics, handball, whatever. Connected with it usually was a swimming tank (natatio).

The dressing room (apodyterium) was entered from the court through a passageway or anteroom; here the bather removed his clothes and placed them in niches provided in the walls—the Pompeian equivalent of our gym lockers. Pictured are the ceiling relief above the entrance to the men's baths in the Forum and the apodyterium of the women's section of the baths (note the magnificent mosaic triton in the floor).

In order to avoid too sudden a temperature change for the bathers, a moderately heated room (tepidarium) was positioned between the dressing room and hot room (caldarium or sudatorium) where hot baths were taken in a tub (solium) or basin (piscina). The caldarium pictured, in the men's bath of the Forum, had a heated floor and walls, the hot air being conducted into a hollow receptacle under the floor and thence via flues between the double walls. A large marble basin (labrum) containing cold water, located at the opposite end of the room, afforded bathers an invigorating cold-dip contrast for head and hands.

From the hot room the bather proceeded to the cold room (frigidarium) for a cold bath. Niccolini's reconstruction of the frigidarium of the Stabian baths pictures the final cold water requisite in the bathing process. Light entered the small circular room through an aperture in the domed ceiling, and water for the circular bath basin fell in a jet from a niche in the upper part of the wall. Some of the larger baths had a separate room called the laconicum for hot dry-air baths, used as a substitute for the hot bath or adding one more hot/cold sequence to the ritual.

After his cold bath, the bather was rubbed down with unguents and scraped with a strigil (a long, narrow scoop-like scraper) to remove the perspiration and smooth and soften the skin. This final operation was usually performed by a tractator (masseur) in the tepidarium. Each bather brought his own gear (towels, unguents and strigils), and loops have been found in Pompeii with strigils and small oil flasks attached for easy wrist-toting.

189

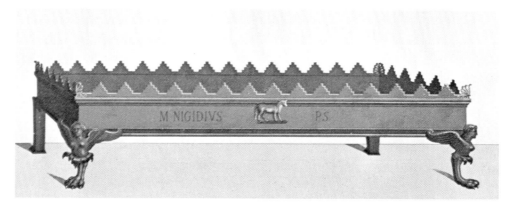

Most residential baths were heated by means of braziers, which could be moved from place to place, such as the one shown here.

Private homes also had their baths, albeit smaller and less complex. The caldarium illustrated is located in the House of the Menander and is considered Pompeii's most sumptuous private bath. The walls were done during the repairs following the earthquake; the floor is older.

191

Classification
Archaeology and Art History, 1880–1945

FREUD'S penetrating analysis of Jensen's Pompeian novel, *Gradiva,* marked the rapid decline of the Pompeian fantasy which had so deeply affected nineteenth-century perceptions of the ancient town. Skillful reconstructions, dependent on Niccolini's great volumes, were still highly prized by collectors and savants alike. Neapolitan firms, such as the Chiurazzi Foundry, prospered making excellent bronze reproductions of statuary from Herculaneum and Pompeii for cultivated, bourgeois tourists, drawn in growing numbers to Campania. But the destructive combination of early twentieth-century scepticism, the rejection of tradition, and the flood of archaeological literature made it increasingly difficult to maintain an image of Classical radiance on the dusty streets of old Pompeii.

The lararium in the home of Lucius Caecilius Jucundus.

Some old-fashioned poets like the American Edgar Fawcett or the German Hermann Lingg could continue to write of the miraculous rebirth of the ancient town, risen for them from the ashes of Vesuvius and rich in the nostalgic experience of a past, lost and regained. Continental novelists, remembering Bulwer-Lytton's success, continued the tradition of the historical novel set in Pompeii, often at a banal level of commercialization, well-represented by Woldemar Kaden in Germany. His countryman H. Lingg's narrative poem, *Clythia. Eine Szene aus Pompeji* (1884), used a Pompeian villa as a backdrop for a sentimental love story which had little to do with Pompeii itself. In like fashion, Otto Behrend wrote *Der Bildhauer. Ein Unterhaltungsroman aus Pompeji* (1907) about a Greek artist, Charmos, who sculpted a statue of Psyche which he finished on the day Vesuvius blew up; his novel ignored Pompeii but had a great deal to say about love, art, and similar noble themes. Even the German archaeologist, Gustav Adolf Müller—another Norbert Hanold—in his novel, *Das sterbende Pompeji* (1910), depended more on nineteenth-century romance, flavored with Bulwer-Lytton, than on the reality of Pompeii which he knew at first hand. Indeed, *The Last Days of Pompeii,* published in 1834, offered a more valid invocation of Pompeii as a setting for the narrative than did any of these successors, including E. Schuré's *La Prêtesse d'Isis: légende de Pompei* (1913) with its distinct, lush echoes of Pierre Louys.

Pompeii, too, came to play roles other than its own. For the writer in the *Catholic World* (volume 69, Jan. 1897), in his article, "Pompeii Reborn and Regenerate," did not concern himself with ancient Pompeii but with the recently depraved modern town, rescued from sin by Divine Grace and by a miraculous picture of the Virgin found in a Naples curio shop; when the picture was placed at the altar of the new church at Valle di Pompeii, it transformed the moral climate of the place—the older Christian gloss on the destruction of Pompeii with a new twist. Equally solemn and earnest is John Hall Ingham's poem, *Pompeii of the West* (1903) with its American locale:

> In the Ausonian land a city rose
> Far from the haunts of poverty and toil,
> Where wearied ones sought rapture and repose,
> And evermore from the enchanted soil
> New fountains flashed into the odorous air,
> New palaces sprang upward to the light,—

Doomed not to know decay: that vision fair
Fled from the wreck of ages,—in a night
Of fire and ashen gloom passed perfect out of sight.

And when the swift-revolving years had brought
Four centuries to a later, larger West,
And men were burdened with the wealth they
    sought,
And Art seemed dying and the Soul oppressed,—
Dawned on our senses in the morning-gleam
That lit the margin of an inland sea
Another city, lovely as a dream,

And like a dream, alas! too soon to be
No more of earth,—a thing of love and memory.

· ·

From the buried past
The shadows of Vesuvian night shall flee,
And, lo, Pompeii—white with Immortality!

Perhaps never before had Pompeii been compared with Chicago.

A sea-change in the attitude of the sensitive visitor to Pompeii may be readily perceived in two accounts of the experience, separated by sixty years. The first is given by Lewis R. Farnell, author of a famous work on comparative religion, *The Cults of the Greek States* (1896–1909), who visited Pompeii in 1886, and the second by Malcolm Lowry, novelist and author of *Under the Volcano* (1947) who came there in 1948:

Farnell:

My days in Pompeii stand out among my life-memories. I had received a private *permesso* to wander about it without guide or guardian; which was invaluable for the true appreciation of the place, as company frustrates one's intercourse with the dead. After a long day's archaeological study, I remained there till the moon had risen and the gates were closed; I had an eerie sense of a haunted city of ghosts as I tried to find an exit through a labyrinth of dim paths and empty courts. In 1886 there was little to be seen of

Gambling and other games—the stone sign announcing the delights within to potential patrons of a Pompeian caupona *(tavern). The dice cup has been given a position of prominence in the middle, with two phalli nicely arranged on each side—hence the downstairs area was devoted to games of chance while erotic activities took place upstairs.*

Herculaneum, and it was only at Pompeii that one could see the outer shell of the ancient life, and more than the shell, something even of the spirit.[1]

And Lowry:

They turned right again into a narrow, rough, and extremely crooked and winding street that had the appearance of going on forever.
'Vico de Lupanare. Wine women and song street,' crowed the guide triumphantly. 'First wine, and afterwards brothel,' he repeated. 'Bread and woman, the first element in life, symbolic . . . All symbolic . . . wait! One entrance—bachelors downstairs; marrieds, priests and the shamefuls upstairs.'
There are, unless you happened to be Toulouse-Lautrec, few things in life less profitable than going to a brothel, unless, Roderick reflected, it was going to a ruined brothel. . . .

Roderick was aware now of a certain blasé obtuseness. Still, a whole street of dead brothels, that had so miraculously survived—relatively—the wrath of God—that was perhaps something to stimulate the lower reaches of the mind after all!

196

Nonetheless Roderick found himself suddenly hating this street with an inexplicable virulence. How he loathed Pompeii! His mouth positively watered with his hatred. Roderick was almost prancing. It seemed to him now that it was as though, by some perverse grace, out of the total inundation of some Pacific Northwestern city, had been preserved a bit of the station hotel, a section of the gasworks, the skeletal remains of four or five palatial cinemas, as many bars and several public urinals, a fragment of marketplace together with the building that once housed the Star Laundries, what was left of several fine industrialists' homes (obscene paintings), a football stadium, the Church of the Four Square Gospel, a broken statue of Bobbie Burns, and finally the remains of the brothels of Chinatown which, though the mayor and police force had labored to have them removed right up to the time of the catastrophe, had nonetheless survived five thousand nine hundred and ninety-nine generations whereupon it was concluded, probably rightly, that the city was one of the seven wonders of the world, as it now stood, but wrongly that anything worthwhile had been there in the first place, with the exception of the mountains. The guide had just said too that even the noise of the traffic had been so deafening in Pompeii that during certain hours they'd had to put a stop to it altogether, as one could well imagine on the stone paved streets—God, how one must have longed to get away! And then he remembered that Pompeii was not a city at all, it was only a small town, by the, by the—[2]

Pompeii's significant loss of position among artists and writers of the twentieth century corresponds to its loss of primacy among archaeologists, drawn away from Campania by the lure of other sites and other excavations. In Italy itself many ancient sites demanded attention, including Rome and the neighboring port city of Ostia Antica; with the unification of Italy archaeological activity spread all over the Italian peninsula and Sicily. The growing range of active excavations and surface explorations quickly extended the volumes of the *Notizie degli Scavi di Antichità* which progressively allotted a smaller share to Pompeii. Peoples and places other than Greek or Roman came to light, especially the mysterious Etruscans who stimulated George Dennis to write his famous *Cities and Cemeteries of Etruria* (1848), prized by traveler, archaeologist, and creative artist alike. Three generations later in 1924 Randall McIver in his *Villanovans and Early Etruscans* could demonstrate the scientific basis for the early history of Italy, founded upon the researches of the great prehistorian, O. Montelius, and his *La Civilisation primitive en Italie* (1895).

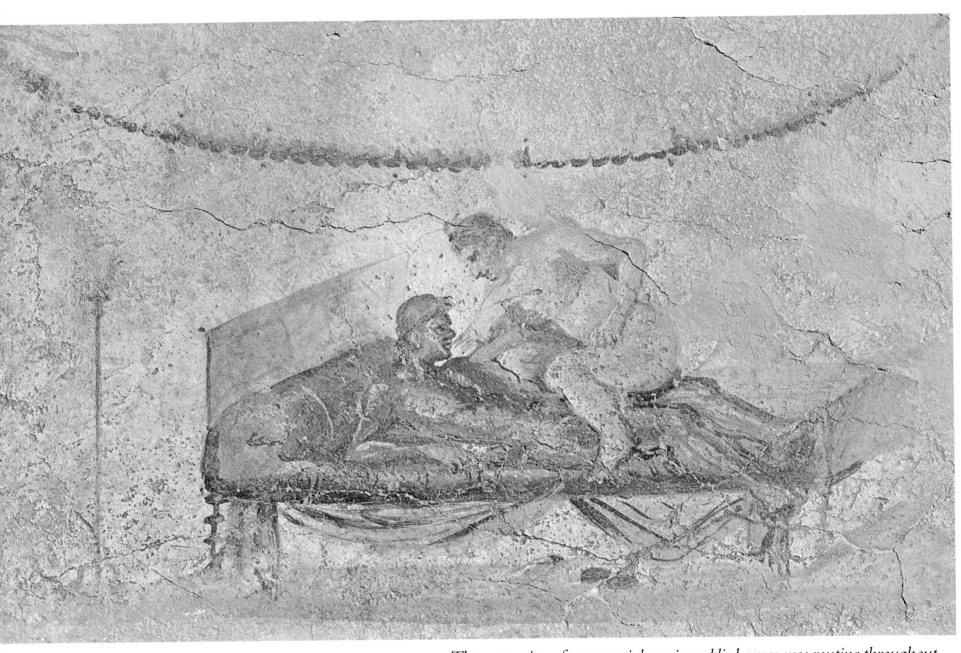

The purveying of commercial sex in public houses was routine throughout the Roman world, and these two illustrations are typical of the graphic lures placed in the love-for-sale lupanare in Pompeii (one was found above the door in a brothel and the other is from the House of the Hunt).

Prehistoric archaeology in Europe also began in the mid-nineteenth century in Scandinavia, Britain, and France. It assumed major proportions when the chronological boundaries of the human presence in the world were vastly extended by two scientists working in separate but cognate fields: Charles Darwin and his *Origin of the Species* (1859) and Charles Lyell, author of *The Geological Evidence of the Antiquity of Man* (1863). In the 1850's and 1860's the accumulation of evidence from long-abandoned caves with human debris and stone implements led to a gradual comprehension of the Paleolithic Period as a pre-historic, pre-civilized state of human existence; the first meeting of the Congrès International d'Anthropologie et d'Archéologie Préhistoriques was held in 1860. Fourteen years later the cave paintings at Altamira in Spain were discovered and the "Art of the Ice Age" became a reality. Other fields of archaeological research soon developed, many of them applied to non-European locales; among them appeared the effort of J. L. Stephens who traveled to Yucatan and Central America in 1840, published his results in 1841, and launched Pre-Columbian archaeology.

The ancient civilizations of the Near East and Egypt, long known through classical and biblical texts and the excited reports of intrepid scholar-adventurers, suddenly became rich fields of archaeological enterprise, often at first taking the familiar form of civilized looting rather than of scientific investigation. Egyptology began with Napoleon's army of the Nile in 1797, with the discovery of the Rosetta Stone, and with Champollion's decipherment of hieroglyphic writing (1821). Egyptian archaeology may be said to start with Mariette's excavations of the Serapaeum at Memphis, quickly followed by A. H. Rhind at Thebes, and in the 1890's by Flinders Petrie, who in 1904 published the classic statement, *Methods and Aims in Archaeology*. Spectacular finds abounded, especially in the painted tombs in the Valley of the Kings near Thebes, but none so spectacular as the Tomb of Tutankhamen, discovered by Howard Carter in 1923.

The Knucklebone Players, a very old painting on marble found in Herculaneum. The two girls in the foreground concentrate on their game, while three others pay scant attention. Knucklebones, incidentally, were made of either real bone or terra cotta.

Mesopotamian archaeology began with Botta at Khorsabad (1843), Layard at Nimrud (1845), and Rawlinson at Behistun in Iran (1846). By 1850 Loftus was excavating at Uruk in lower Mesopotamia, 1860 Renan in Phoenicia, 1873 Smith in Assyria, 1884 Dieulafoy at Susa, 1880's Sayce in Hittite Anatolia, 1887 the Americans at Nippur, and so on. In 1926 Charles Woolley discovered the Royal Tombs at Ur and Mesopotamian archaeology also had its spectacular, golden find to complement all the slabs of relief sculpture taken from Assyrian palaces and from Persepolis to adorn the walls of European and American museums. Equally important was the establishment of the Palestine Exploration Fund in 1866 in the service of biblical archaeology, a service it has performed for more than a century.

More spectacular than any of these, at least for classically educated Europeans, were the discoveries of a German businessman, Heinrich Schliemann, an amateur of Homer, who sought to find the ancient places known to Homer but lost to history. In 1869 Schliemann excavated in Ithaca, the home island of Odysseus, and ever the publicist he published his results in the same year. In 1871 he began his excavations at Troy which he published three years later, to the astonishment of all; this was followed by his dig at Mycenae in 1874, published in 1876, and in 1884 he began work at nearby Tiryns. Apart from the splendor of his discoveries and the extraordinary demonstration of the Homeric world which he conjured up from these ruins, thus transforming an historical phantom into fact, Schliemann created a new field of archaeology: Mycenaean or Bronze Age archaeology. This field was quickly put on a scientific basis by sober German scholars like Dörpfeld who published his *Troja* in 1894 and went around in Schliemann's footsteps, moderating his enthusiastic attributions and setting the discoveries more soundly on the basis of stratigraphic analysis.

Nevertheless, Madame Schliemann's portrait, wearing on her generous bosom the gold ornaments from Mycenae, made a great impression. A few years later, stimulated by these preclassical discoveries in the eastern Mediterranean and by Schliemann's faith in the historicity of the Homeric texts, Arthur Evans began his excavations at Knossos in 1900. Those excavations culminated in his discovery of the long-lost, unknown civilization of the Minoans, published in his magisterial *Palace of Minos* (1921–1935), and indicating a non-Greek presence in the Bronze Age world of the Aegean.

Archaeologists at work in Pompeii in the latter part of the 19th century.

Scientific bodies, often the archaeological extension of state systems of education, entered the field and established continuing programs of excavation at specific sites: in 1875 the Germans began their excavations at Olympia, in 1877 the French at Delos, in the 1880's the Germans at Pergamon and the Austrians at Ephesos. Soon, many national institutions, American included, were deeply engaged in semi-permanent excavations, dependent on concessions given by host countries which after World War I became increasingly restricted and restrictive. These continuing excavations—e.g. the Germans at Olympia and Pergamon, the French at Delos and Delphi, the Italians in Libya and Crete, the English in Crete, the French in Tunisia and Algeria, the Americans at Corinth and Athens, etc.—took on a life of their own, greatly enriching our knowledge of the past and presenting new insights and points of entry into the ancient world of the Mediterranean.

In this welter of competing archaeological sites—many of them novel, splendid in their rising ruins, and major centers of ancient civilization—Pompeii came to be considered somewhat declassé. Pompeii lost its long-held archaeological franchise because it was, after all, not so old as Knossos or Mycenae, not so special as Olympia or Delphi, not so grand as Pergamon or Ephesos, and not so representative of the glorious classical past as Athens or Rome. Indeed, Julius Lessing, writing a book with August Mau on a recently discovered Roman house on the Tiber bank in Rome in 1891—the so-called Villa Farnesina—stated his pleasure that finally Roman wall-painting could be studied in its true light at the capital and not in a provincial town like Pompeii.

What then was left for Pompeian archaeology? Apparently a great deal, but no longer in the guise of a pace-setter in Classical archaeology nor as an idealized exemplum of antique civilization. Rather, Pompeii came to be appreciated more for itself as the gloss of romance and representation wore off, and in doing so the character of its ancient community, of its ancient urban structure emerged more clearly.

The history of Pompeian archaeology from 1880 to 1945 can be broken into two distinct periods, divided by Vittorio Spinazzola's accession to the directorship in 1910. The earlier period followed the pattern of excavation and report set out by Fiorelli but with some new priorities. The directors—Michele Ruggiero, Giulio de Petra, Ettore Pais, and Antonio Sogliano—were increasingly concerned with the conservation and restoration of the excavated structures, an especially pressing problem in view of the

View of the Via dell'Abbondanza with the inscribed public notices clearly visible on the front of the House of Aulus Trebius Valens (by Spinazzola).

205

rapid pace of excavation and the popularity of the site for tourists. They also intensified their interest in stratigraphical studies of the periods before and after A.D. 79 and began to reach beyond the walls of the town to explore the *ager Pompeianus,* the exurban territory belonging to Pompeii, and the suburban villas on the slopes of Vesuvius to the northeast.

1880

Work continued in the ninth region, insulae 7 and 8; in *1881,* shifted to the south side of the Strada dell'Abbondanza in the eighth region, insulae 5 and 6; in *1884* workmen reached VIII-7.

1884

J. A. Overbeck and A. Mau published *Pompeji in seinen Gebäuden, Alterthümern und Kunstwerken* (Leipzig) which included for the first time the scale model of Pompeii housed in the Naples Museum; the model, made by Vincenzo Bramante and sons, was completed by 1899 and has not been extended since.

1885

House of Joseph II (VIII-2-38) excavated, named after the Emperor of Austria.

1886

Excavations on the *Via di Nocera,* outside the walls near the amphitheater; work on VIII-2 continued sporadically to *1890.*

1889

The *Stabian Gate* was freed.

F. von Duhn and L. Jacobi investigated the stratigraphy in the area of the Greek Temple in the *Triangular Forum;* together they published *Der Griechische Tempel in Pompeji* (Heidelberg, 1890).

1892–93

Houses along the *Strada di Nola* cleared (V-2-6, 9, 13, 17); work continued outside the *Stabian Gate.*

*The beginning of the Via dell'Abbondanza beside the Building of
Eumachia. The large stone obstructions in the foreground are to block traffic
from entering the Forum from the street.*

The Nolan Gate and its outer wall defensive works.

1893

Giulio de Petra became director of excavations to 1900, and again from 1906 to 1910.
House of the Silver Wedding (V–2) excavated and named in honor of the wedding anniversary of the King and Queen of Italy; perhaps the most splendid private house in Pompeii after the House of the Faun; it was preserved largely through the efforts of M. Ruggiero.

1894

Work continued on the tombs of the *Strada Stabiana*.
House of the Vettii (VI-15-1) excavated, and fully cleared by 1895; 188 paintings found in the house were left in place as the house and its garden were carefully restored to preserve the original environment of its rich, merchant-class owners.

Plan of the House of the Vettii

1. *Vestibule*
2. *Atrium*
3. *Staircase to upper story*
4. *Kitchen*
5. *Dining room (triclinium)*
6. *Dining room (triclinium, "Pentheus Room")*
7. *Peristyle garden*
8. *Oecus*
9. *Small peristyle*
10. *Dining room/sitting room*
11. *Bedroom*

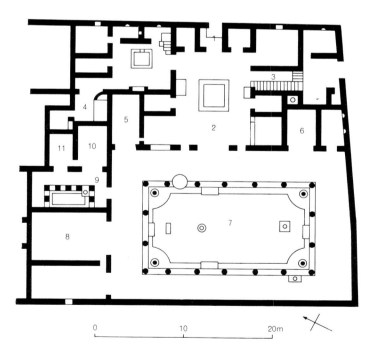

A perspective of the Pentheus Room in the House of the Vettii, so named because its most prominent painting depicts Pentheus being torn limb from limb by maenads. There is also a painting of Hercules as a baby engaged in quelling serpents plus two lovely panels containing paintings of pavilions that have an almost Oriental aspect.

A wall of the Ixion Room in the House of the Vettii. The painting portrays Daedalus (the great mythological inventor) presenting Pasiphaë (wife of King Minos of Crete) with a life-size wooden cow. Poseidon had caused her to become enamored with a bull, and at her request Daedalus created this ingenious means by which she could mate with it (there was a small trap door in the back of the hollow inside). The outcome of this coupling was the monstrous Minotaur with the head of a bull and the body of a man.

211

Cupid riding a crab, a charming wall painting located in the atrium of the House of the Vettii.

212

Peristyle and garden of the House of the Golden Cupids.

1894–1900

Excavations of Roman villas at Boscoreale on the side of Vesuvius, northeast of Pompeii, begun after a false start in 1876. Contents of these villas widely distributed to major art museums: *Treasure of Boscoreale*—consisting of gold and silver pieces, elegant silver tableware, and more than 1,000 gold coins—mostly purchased by Baron de Rothschild and given to the Louvre; other vessels of glass, bronze, and silver, bronze furniture and bathtubs in the Field Museum, Chicago; wall-paintings from the Villa of P. Fannius Synistor broken up with lion's share going to the Metropolitan Museum, New York. *Villa at Boscotrecase,* nearby, also excavated in *1902* with numerous wall-paintings also distributed, some in the Metropolitan Museum in New York. Ironically, of the more than 1,000 paintings discovered in Pompeii or in its region from 1875 to 1900 more fell into private or non-Italian hands than went to the Naples Museum, although the majority were retained in place, given the new theory of conservation. Laws controlling the exportation of national (archaeological and artistic) treasures were not yet in effect.

1895

House of the Golden Cupids (VI-16-7) excavated; completed in 1905 and ambience of an upper-class house well preserved.

Pompeian panorama from the Vesuvian Gate with the Sarno Valley and Lattari mountains in the background (an Anderson photograph).

1895–97

Insula VI-15 cleared all the way to city wall.

1897/9

City wall between towers X–XI cleared.

A. Mau & F. W. Kelsey published *Pompeii, its Life and Art* (New York).

1899–1901

Private excavation conducted by G. Matrone south of Pompeii toward coast and harbor where maritime villa discovered, called (erroneously) *Villa of Cicero.*

1900

Work in insulae IV-7, and 10; V-4 and 5, VI-12 and 15, VII-5, and 7, and 15, VIII-2, IX-6; also in area of *Forum* and *Temple of Jupiter,* and outside wall to north.

Exploration of system of drains undertaken.

1901

Ettore Pais made director of Naples Museum and Pompeian excavations; clearing operations in regions V, VI.

1901–02

Clearing of *Vesuvian Gate.*

Detail of a wall painting found in the dining hall of the Villa at Boscoreale
(supposedly the lady is the mother of Antigonos Gonatas).

Lady playing the cithara, a wall painting from the Villa at Boscoreale belonging to The Metropolitan Museum of Art.

216

*Idyllic sacred landscape originally located on the
wall of the red oecus in the Villa of Agrippa
Postumus at Boscotrecase.*

1903

Excavation of water-tower near Vesuvian Gate and in region VI, most notably the *House of the Ara Maxima* (VI-15-16), important for the cult of Hercules. Patrician *House of Obellius Firmus* (IX-10-1) opened, actively excavated 1905–1911; possesses largest four-columned atrium in Pompeii.

1903–04

Clearing of area of *Vesuvian Gate* and part of the *Strada Stabiana* from that gate along VI-16.

Charles Waldstein attempted to develop an international consortium to reopen the excavations of Herculaneum, long dormant; for reasons of politics and nationalism it failed and excavations of Herculaneum recommenced only in *1927*.

Charles Waldstein published *Herculaneum. Past, Present and Future* (London, 1908) with its record of past achievement and a program for future work.

1905–06

Villa of the Mosaic Columns on the Street of Tombs outside the Herculaneum Gate excavated together with several small tombs on the opposite side of the street. The *House of the Gladiators* (V-5-3) was opened, as well as several cisterns in regions V and VI. Final clearing of the *House of the Golden Cupids.*

Antonio Sogliano director, 1905–1910.

1906

Completion of Dörpfeld and Mau's examination of the stage of the *Great Theater* at Pompeii, begun in 1902.

1907

Work resumed on the *House of the Silver Wedding* (V-2-1).

Excavation in cemeteries to the south and east of town.

1908–09

Excavation and survey of areas outside the Nolan and Vesuvian Gates; garden of the *House of the Queen of Holland* (V-3-7) cleared and also in the *House of the Duchess of Aosta* (V-3-13).

1909–10

Partial excavation of the *Villa of the Mysteries* (Villa Item), largely by its owner Sig. Item; set aside and not resumed until 1929/30 when the Villa was fully cleared and its splendid architecture and monumental paintings revealed, the latter giving their name to the Villa—see A. Maiuri, *La Villa dei Misteri* (2 volumes, Rome, 1931).

1910

Spinazzola became director.

Information about the ongoing archaeological activity at Pompeii from 1880 to 1910 is derived largely from Mau's articles in the *Bollettino dell'Istituto* and, beginning in 1886, its successor the *Römische Mitteilungen*, as well as from unsigned articles in the *Notizie degli Scavi*; after 1900 those articles were signed, usually by A. Sogliano, G. Spano, or M. della Corte. Mau's articles and the *Notizie* complemented each other, and both must be used to recover the history of Pompeian archaeology in this period.

Mau constantly stressed the importance of systematic analysis and presentation. Each building in an insula was described, and buildings were taken in order around a block, sometimes accompanied by a brief discussion of the history of the insula or of its building phases. Houses were described room by room with especial attention to techniques of construction, phases of rebuilding or alteration, decorative schemes of rooms, and plans, with measurements of rooms often provided. From 1878 Mau sometimes gave the plan of the insulae, and from 1893 he used reconstructed cross-sections and perspective drawings of houses, complementing the longer and more detailed descriptions of the buildings. Mau relied heavily on his own categories of Four Styles in defining the decorative schemes, but still gave great attention to the large subject paintings; when these paintings were removed, because of his own interest in the ensemble Mau provided a record of their original position. In sum, Mau tried to organize the evidence into some meaningful structure.

The articles in the *Notizie* depended on Mau's synthetic analysis. They concentrated instead on reporting the excavator's journal, often summarized rather briefly and filled with a record of finds; occasionally several similar objects were lumped together making later identification very difficult. After 1900 the reports in the *Notizie* continued as before, a catalogue of finds ordered by day of discovery, modified by the need to present a coherent topographical description. The catalogue of finds was sometimes preceded by a description of a building or group of paintings which reflected a greater awareness of context; thus the description of the *House of Lucretius Fronto* (V–4–11) in 1901 which included a plan and also photographs of the interior, or that of the *House of the Golden Cupids* whose quality warranted extended treatment in the *Notizie* of 1906, 1907. Matters of special interest got particularized attention, as well: the system of drains in 1900, the water-tower by the Vesuvian Gate and its involvement in water distribution (1903), Mau's investigation of the Theater in 1906, and a discussion of the street ensemble, including paving, sidewalks, and inscriptions, also in 1906.

The fragmentary character of the evidence and its very rapid accumulation required new methods of organization, and the natural model was Pompeii itself, a coherent urban structure. Following Fiorelli's lead, block-clearing operations came to dominate archaeological activity and with it the orderly uncovering of the street network, including avenues, side-streets, and narrow, connecting alleyways. To make sense of what was found, plans of individual structures or of areas, even entire insulae, became essential; with plans came architectural sections which could suggest the three-dimensional reality of the buildings. Then the ground-work was laid for an extensive program of reconstruction, the restorations effected so sensitively by Ruggiero, de Petra, and Antonio Sogliano of parts of buildings—a portico, atrium, columned peristyle, or garden—and of buildings as a whole and their relationship to adjacent streets; thus, the rebuilding of the overhanging balconies of the Brothel on the street which carries the appropriate name, *Vico del Balcone pensile* (Street of the Hanging Balcony) and a similarly named House (VII-12-28). Everything was ready for the enthusiastic arrival of Spinazzola who saw Pompeii as archaeological theater, an environment for recreating the physical conditions of the ancient town by the employment of the most careful techniques of recovery, ordered by a vivid and coherent picture of the primary locus of Pompeian life, the street. And the street he chose was the *Via dell'Abbondanza*.

Excavation work at the House of Marcus Lucretius Fronto in 1900 (an Alinari photograph).

Narcissus, son of the river-god Cephissus in Greek mythology, was possessed of a surpassing beauty. His mother was told that he would have a long life, provided he never looked upon his own features. After rejecting the love of the nymph Echo, he was punished by the goddess of love who caused him to fall in love with his own reflection when he knelt to drink beside a spring and subsequently pine away. The flower that bears his name is said to have sprung up where he died and was thought to be a symbol of death. The painting of Narcissus gazing at his own watery image to the left graces the wall in the cubiculum to the right of the tablinum in the handsome House of Marcus Lucretius Fronto pictured above. As a further note, Echo fared no better than the object of her affections. She was deprived of speech, except for the power to repeat the last words of another, and then as a result of her unrequited love for Narcissus faded away to a voice only.

*Spinazzola view of the Via dell'Abbondanza, showing the inscriptions on
the walls and balcony, the Tavern of the Four Divinities (Apollo, Jupiter,
Mercury and Diana), a thermopolium and the oblong street stones.*

Spinazzola methodically excavated both sides of the Via dell'Abbondanza, the
town's principal commercial thoroughfare, from 1910 to 1923. This deliberate program
was followed by his distinguished successor, Amadeo Maiuri, from 1924 to 1941, until
the street—bordered by regions I and II on the south, IX and III on the north—ran clear
from the Strada Stabiana eastward to the Sarno Gate. The entire reality of the ancient
strip opened to sight and to movement, giving to the passerby an unprecedented "feel"
of Pompeii as it was because the lively interaction between continuous strip and active

façade became directly available to him. In the annals of Pompeian archaeology this area is known as the "New Excavations" for reasons explained in A. W. Van Buren's article marking the appearance of Spinazzola's great posthumous work, *Pompei alla Luce degli Scavi Nuovi di Via dell'Abbondanza*:

The systematic excavation of Pompeii dates from the year 1748; and for the greater part of two centuries the houses were uncovered by the simple process of removing first the modern soil and then the *ejecta . . .* from the eruption of A.D. 79 together with such fragmentary debris from the upper parts of the houses as might still be surviving mixed with the volcanic matter. Attention was concentrated on the painted walls and the valuable works of art in the ground-floor rooms. The results appear in the older, long familiar publications. These convey an inadequate, largely conjectural impression of the upper parts of the houses, and in particular they offer little evidence as to upper-story balconies and windows, or upper-story planning in general, and not the slightest suggestion of the sloping roofs which overhung the sidewalks and protected the gaily painted fronts of the houses from sun and rain.

The tools of the smithy trade flanking a good-luck, protective phallus proclaim the occupation of L. Livius Firmus. This relief is located in the wall to the right of the entrance to his establishment. The sledge hammer, tongs and phallus are painted a brilliant red.

Sign on the side of a bottega including a refreshing little replica of Mercury, Via dell'Abbondanza (a 1935 Alinari photograph).

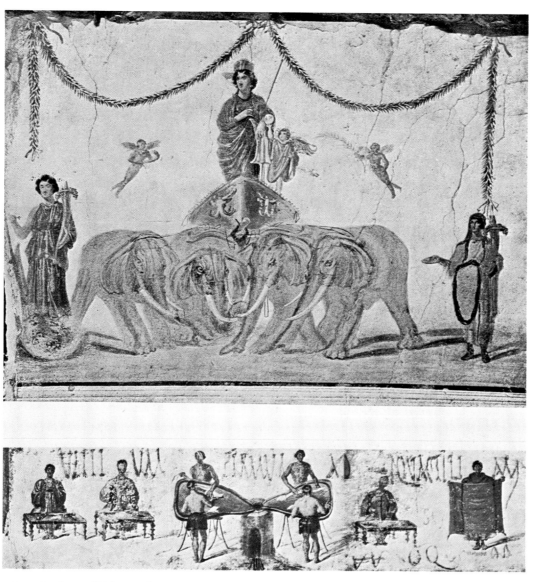

A painting of Venus Pompeiana, patroness of Pompeii, standing atop an elephant quadriga, appears above the shop sign of the cloth factory and salesroom of M. Vecilius Verecundus on the Via dell'Abbondanza (by Spinazzola).

When Vittorio Spinazzola became director of the excavations in 1910, his primary objective was to remedy this defect—to recover material evidence as to the nature of the upper stories. At neighboring Herculaneum such elements had been preserved by reason of their being encased in the torrents of volcanic mud that engulfed the city; but the excavators had paid slight attention to them; . . . Spinazzola reasoned that the remains of upper stories at Pompeii must surely be in existence, buried among the layers formed in that city by the successive phases of the great eruption, with their concomitant earthquake shocks. Tile roofs and the collapsed upper parts of walls and columns should be found lying exactly where they had fallen, awaiting only the well-trained eye and observant mind of the excavator to be recognized and interpreted and to be restored to their original positions. He decided to apply this new method to the clearing of a stretch of one of the main thoroughfares of the city; and he trained his capable staff of workers to remove the layers of *ejecta*, proceeding downward from the modern ground level, little by little, carefully observing, saving and replacing each fragment in a framework which eventually was incorporated in a reconstruction, in durable materials, of the original fabric. He also impressed upon them the need for preserving the countless bits of stucco from the surfaces of walls and ceilings with a view to reassembling these and thus, as far as possible, recovering the paintings that formed a special adornment of the house interiors. With this went the re-erection and preservation of the many-colored façades, a revelation of the aspect of the city and its testimony to the outdoor life and interests of the inhabitants. . . .[3]

Spinazzola's book is itself a primer for instructing the reader in the new method of scientific excavation at an historical site. With ample illustrations—plans, drawings, reconstructions, and photographs—he provides a compendium of the evidence for critical review, while demonstrating the effectiveness of the method by the closest attention to detail. Part I, entitled "Architetture della Strada," presents Spinazzola's view of the street as a primary structure, carefully shaped by the buildings on its flanks and by the very fact of linear extension. Chapter I embodies his theory and method of excavation, incorporating a useful review of the history of past excavation at Pompeii and Herculaneum and stating explicitly his objectives in excavation:

1. To discover and define the street as the primary objective of archaeological research at Pompeii and to analyze the structure and organization of the façades that line the street. Thus he transferred the traditional concern over the interior (and interiors) of

the house to the exterior, because that is where the urban relationship is to be found.

2. To discover the "lost" upper stories of the street-flanking structures because it is necessary to do so in order to reconstruct the façades correctly in their full elevation and thus in their full relation to the street and to the opposite façades; doing so would also assist in the reconstruction of the interior of buildings.

3. To establish a method of systematic excavation by stratum in order to control the recovery of data, otherwise destroyed in the process of excavation, and to maintain a continual photographic record as one digs down to serve as a control and as the only historical evidence of the legitimacy of the archaeologist's conclusions or reconstructions, once the stratigraphy is disturbed.

4. To relearn the ancient techniques of construction and of making so as to be able to recognize their traces in the debris, to respect their character and limitations without modernization, and to understand how to duplicate them effectively in reliable reconstructions.

Chapters II–V in Part I demonstrate how Spinazzola could apply his method successfully to reconstruct the ancient roofs and roof-line, upper-story windows, balconies, and porches, and the mezzanines over shop fronts. None of this had been done before nor had it been possible to rebuild the upper stories of these buildings with any degree of confidence; now it could be done. The present appearance of the Via dell'Abbondanza testifies to his achievement as do the modern reconstructions of Ostia Antica.

Part II of his book, entitled "Colori della Strada," addresses the painted decorations of the façades and arranges them by subject: history pictures, religious paintings which refer to the great gods or to the lesser but popular cults, and the signs, the latter of all kinds including political slogans, electioneering, and scurrilous graffiti. Indirectly, this colorful street decoration preserves the color of street life itself. Part III presents seriatim a number of important houses with preserved upper floors, discovered by Spinazzola in his excavation of the street-ribbon and thoroughly dug out behind the façade; each of them appears in a miniature monograph, complete with plans, views, and reconstructed. Altogether, Spinazzola was the true heir of Niccolini, a visionary of the past, but established on a firm archaeological foundation which gave substance to his colorful dreams.

The prosiac work of excavation went on with impressive regularity, and was reported in the *Notizie*:

1911

Work continued in the *House of Obellius Firmus* (IX–10–1), formerly known as the House of the Count of Turin. Spinazzola's venture extended beyond the borders of the Via dell'Abbondanza.

1912–19

Excavations along both sides of the *Via dell'Abbondanza*, slowed by the advent of war.

1915

House of Trebius Valens (III–2–1) begun and continued until 1916.

1916

Samnite-Roman necropolis outside Stabian Gate dug.

In the period 1911 to 1919 reports in the *Notizie* were given by M. della Corte and G. Spano in the conventional way, dependent on Spinazzola's field notes for the

The colorful square wall decoration in the House of Aulus Trebius Valens on the Via dell'Abbondanza.

230

The back of this highly polished hand mirror, part of the celebrated silver cache found in the House of the Menander, is decorated with a separately made emblem of a profile of a female head. The clear delineation and precision of craftsmanship are strongly reminiscent of that found on Greek coins, although the form and ornamentation of the mirror itself are without question Roman.

231

major activity on the Via dell'Abbondanza. Where groups of skeletons were found together, as in the garden of the *House of the Cryptoporticus* (I-6-4), Spinazzola attempted to reconstruct the circumstances of their deaths (1914). In the excavation of the Roman and Samnite cemetery, the burials were listed separately. On the whole, the reports preserved a matter-of-fact tone, quite removed from Spinazzola's ambitious reconstructions.

1921–23

Work continued on the *Via dell'Abbondanza* and in the larger houses along the street. Spinazzola retired from the directorship and was briefly succeeded by Minto.

1924

Amadeo Maiuri became director and remained in this position until *1961*. From 1924 to 1941 he continued the progressive excavations along the Via dell'Abbondanza.

M. della Corte published *I nuovi scavi (case ed abitanti)* (Naples).

1924–26

Work continued on I-7 in an effort to clear the insula and neared completion in 1927.

1927

House of Paquius Proculus (I-7-1) completely uncovered as well as *House of Publius Tegete* (I-7-11). Insula I-6 fully cleared.

1927

Excavations begun again at *Herculaneum* after more than a century of inactivity.

1928–31

Excavation of the system of water pipes.

Maiuri published the first edition of his synthetic *Pompei* (Novara, 1928), in all its editions and translations the most popular general work on Pompeii ever written.

1929–30

The *Villa of the Mysteries* was fully cleared and published (Maiuri, 1931); all wall-paintings were retained in situ including the *Frieze of the Dionysiac Mysteries*, perhaps the most important of all Pompeian paintings.

1930–31

House of the Menander (I-10-4) discovered, fully excavated with its rich treasure of silver—see A. Maiuri, *La casa del Menandro e il suo tesoro di argentaria* (2 volumes, Rome, 1933).

1931–34

Insula I-10 cleared fully.

This garden painting of a white stork picking at a lizard, a pet dog and a large green plant from the House of the Epigrams is very similar to a painting found in the peristyle of the House of the Menander.

1932
Work resumed on clearing the *Via dell'Abbondanza* its full length, achieved by 1935. A. Maiuri in *Pompei, I nuovi scavi* (Rome), in Italian, French, English, and German, singled out the "New Excavations" for special, individual treatment for the benefit of the tourist.

1933–35
Clearing of the Via dell'Abbondanza extended southeast toward *Amphitheater* and *Palaestra*, fronts of six insulae on the *Via dell'Abbondanza* (III–5, 6, and 7; II–5, 6, and 7) cleared, consistent with Spinazzola's original program.

More tombs on the *Street of Tombs* freed, especially in the area of the *Villa of the Mosaic Columns.*

The Forum with Vesuvius in the background. The depth and scope of this structural complex gains perspective with the figure of the lone visitor (an Alinari photograph).

The colossal columns of the Great Palaestra located west of the Amphitheater. Three sides were closed off by a portico, the fourth by a wall. Inside this broad rectangular expanse was a huge swimming pool sheltered by a double row of plane trees.

1933–1935

Long-standing major project, clearing the city walls, pushed hard in *1934–35*, freeing the line from the *Herculaneum Gate* to *Tower XI* to the *Vesuvian Gate.*

1935–39

Palaestra near Amphitheater fully excavated and restored; many bodies found in portico.

1935–41

Return to older excavated sites for purpose of intense stratigraphic exploration, seeking out pre-Roman and pre-Samnite levels, as well as defining the shape of the pre-Roman town; test pits dug in the area of the *Forum*—Building of Eumachia, the Macellum, Temple of Vespasian, Curia, and Temple of Jupiter—complementing earlier trials (1931) in the precinct of Apollo, turned up potshards of the sixth and fifth centuries B.C.

1936

Clearing out of Region VIII between the *Forum* and the zone of the *Triangular Forum* and *Theaters,* thus opening connection between two principal urban centers.

1940

Mussolini entertained the German Minister of Education in the dining room of the recently reconstructed *House of the Menander.*

1943

Excavation of the foundations of many houses, including that of the *Great Fountain* (VI-8-22) and of *Pansa* (VI-6-1), in order to examine the foundations of the oldest buildings, as had been done at the *House of the Surgeon* (VI-1-9) in 1930.

On *August 24*, and on *September 13* and *26* Allied bombs fell on Pompeii striking several houses on the *Via dell'Abbondanza* cleared by Spinazzola and Maiuri only a few years before. The *Antiquarium* was almost totally destroyed, revealing part of a great suburban villa with a large triclinium; this early Imperial villa had been damaged in the earthquake of A.D. 62 and was being demolished in 79. The bombing also revealed a *Sanctuary of Dionysus* with Roman and pre-Roman levels outside the walls in the area of S. Abbondio.

April 13, Spinazzola died; in August, the warehouse of the Italian publishing house of Hoepli in Milan was bombed and with it the sheets of Spinazzola's book on the Via dell'Abbondanza, waiting for binding.

1944

Vesuvius erupted for several months.

1948

Antiquarium of Pompeii was reopened on June 13 in celebration of the second centenary of the excavations.

Located on the outskirts of Pompeii, the Villa of the Mysteries derives its name from the remarkable frescoes pictured here—a free-flowing panoramic frieze featuring great figured compositions in a continuing sweep around the walls. The photo below of the entire north wall and a portion of the east wall lends a perspective to the scope of this ritualistic portrayal. When first uncovered in 1930, the frieze caused an artistic furor, and through the years its meaning has continued to confound the experts. The pieces of the puzzle are presented on the following pages.

North wall, first scene. The bride [or initiate] walks toward the threshold (left); the preparations [or rites] are about to begin. A small nude boy reads what is probably a sacred text from a scroll under the guidance of a seated woman [his mother?] who holds a stylus in one hand and another scroll in the other. A third woman, wearing a wreath of olive leaves and carrying an olive branch and what appears to be a tray of cakes, looks out as she walks toward the second scene.

North wall, second scene. A priestess, seated with her back to the viewer, removes a cloth from a basket held by a feminine attendant while another attendant pours purifying water over her right hand. Gazing off toward the third scene—and really a part of that sequence—a no-longer-young Silenus fingers his lyre which he has propped against a small supporting column.

239

North wall, third scene. A youthful satyress suckles a goat, while a billy goat stands by. In the forefront in an attitude of alarm, a woman appears to be warding off some unknown evil—by pushing whatever it is away with one hand and by placing some protective covering over her head with the other.

240

East wall, first scene. Proponents of the Dionysian theme of the frieze point to this sequence as the proof of the pudding. A young satyr gazes as if mesmerized into a bowl held by another Silenus, while a second satyr holding a theatrical mask aloft looks on. (Note the disapproving look that Silenus seems to be giving to the frightened lady in the previous scene.) Next to this group—and dominating the wall—Dionysus lies sprawled in loving abandon in the arms of Ariadne (conjecture since this part of the frieze is sadly ruined) who appears to be sitting on some sort of throne.

241

East wall, second scene. A kneeling woman with a long torch over her shoulder prepares to unveil some purple-shrouded object [held by many to be a ritual phallus]. The purpose of the winnowing basket at her feet is unknown. To her right a female figure with dark wings spread endeavors to shut out the previous sequence with one hand as she raises her whip in the other to strike the young woman in the next scene.

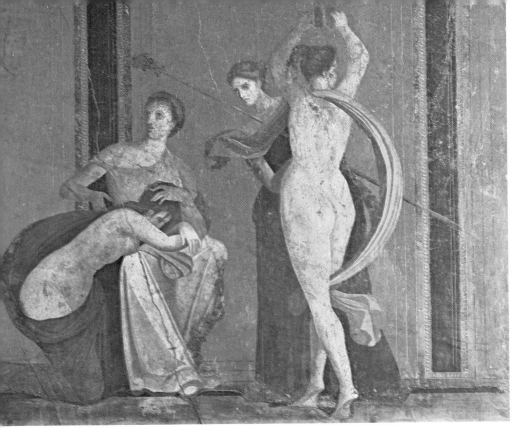

South wall, first scene. The two essential movements of the ritual—torture and transfiguration—are evocatively climaxed in this scene depicting the flogging of a young woman who lays sprawled across the lap of her companion. The utter abandonment to agony written on her face is poignantly expressed in the detail from this scene below. To the right a naked woman clashes her cymbals in delight as a fully clothed female extends what appears to be a thyrsus, symbolic wand of Dionysus.

South wall, second scene. All agree that this scene portrays the bride's toilet, but whether she is a bride in a religious or human sense is not clear. An attendant arranges her hair while an obliging Eros holds her mirror.

West wall, final scene. Mother of the bride? Perhaps the bride herself? (She does wear a ring on her finger.) Or possibly the mistress of the villa contemplating the frieze? No one can say with certainty since so many of the elements in the episodes are hidden from our eyes. And in the last analysis, it is the fascination of not knowing that lends the final enchantment to this endlessly intriguing frieze.

Carbonized cradle, found in Herculaneum.

As usual, much of the information about the excavations from 1921 to 1945 depends on the *Notizie degli Scavi*, with M. della Corte publishing the epigraphic material and Maiuri everything else. The principal investigators also tended to supplement their reports with numerous articles in both foreign and domestic journals as well as in monographic studies that began to appear in the mid 1920's. Because of the hiatus in excavation and reporting during World War I, the early post-war numbers of the *Notizie* reviewed some of the older digs, especially the excavation of suburban villas

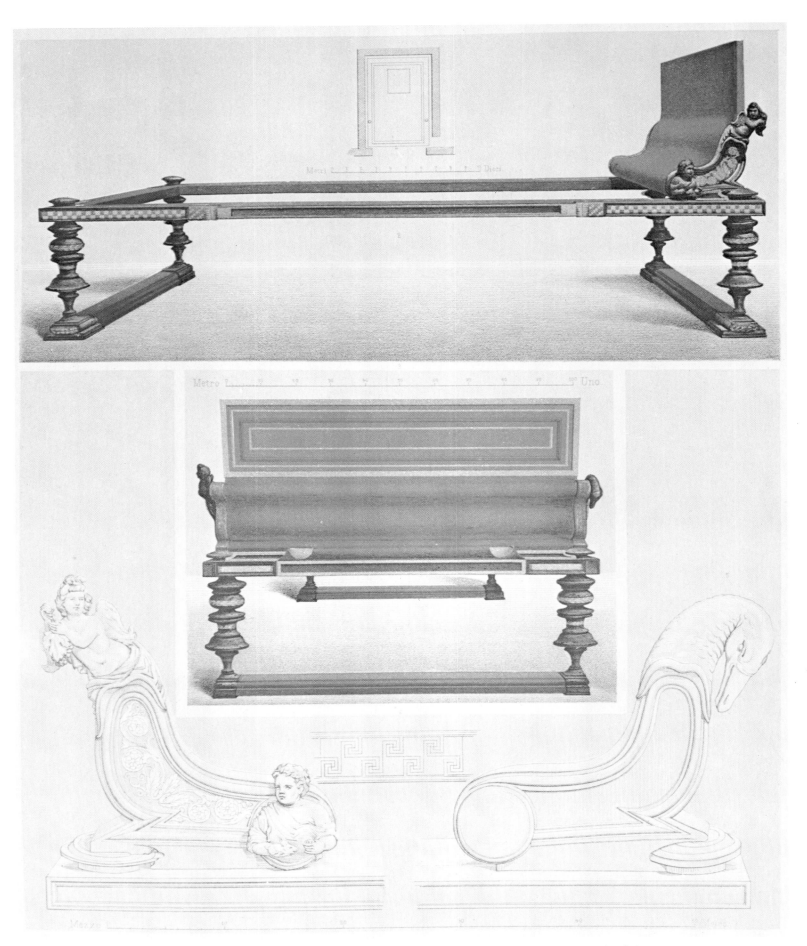

Pompeians dined on couches while supporting themselves via the left elbow. Here is a colorful dining couch and other re-created furniture by Niccolini.

on private lands outside of Pompeii. Soon, however, Maiuri asserted his own interests and in his first report (1927) criticized his mentor, Spinazzola, for the policy of excavating in depth only those houses along the Via dell'Abbondanza that seemed to be particularly impressive—a vestige of the old elitist attitude. Maiuri took the position that he would try to recover neighborhoods as organic wholes, including all the elements that constitute an insula, but he was still attracted by quality and opulence in his finds.

Maiuri and della Corte sought to lay bare both the architectural and social structure of each neighborhood, thereby illustrating the mixed use and mixed company which characterizes so much of Pompeii, especially in the area of the Via dell'Abbondanza. Therefore, the reports of the period from 1924 to 1933 published the current excavations with even greater thoroughness than before. General descriptions of the architecture were supported by analyses of building techniques, efforts were made to date the parts of buildings as well as the whole, and the archaeologists tried to estimate the social status of the owners, using the evidence provided by inscriptions, occupations, and the quality of interior decoration and furnishings. For these reasons a room-by-room description of an excavated house was especially detailed; finds were listed at the end of the account, including miscellaneous objects and inscriptions, while more and more photographs complemented the verbal description of works of art. With this view

Looking west over Region VI of Pompeii from a tower along the city walls.

*View over Herculaneum offering a visual depth-study of the burial brought
on by the A.D. 79 eruption.*

in mind, Maiuri in 1933 resumed working on the Via dell'Abbondanza, intending to clear the entire length of the street to the Sarno Gate; and he did so. The large southeast quarter of town between the Sarno Gate and the Nucerian Gate, a zone dominated by the amphitheater and the palaestra, was also scheduled for clearance, and that too was accomplished for the most part.

The reports offered extended digressions into specific concerns of the excavators, aroused by scholarly interests of general applicability or by the chances of discovery. Thus, the uncovering of a well near the water-tower of the Vesuvian Gate in 1928 led to an extended study of the system of wells and pipes throughout Pompeii, and of its development; public wells apparently predated a system of water distribution, dependent on aqueducts, but once the water pipes were installed, wells like the one beside the Vesuvian Gate became private suppliers of water. Similarly, the extensive explorations of and around the amphitheater produced a long report in 1939 which thoroughly reviewed its architectural history, using as evidence of its late appearance the painting of the riot in the amphitheater of 59 A.D.; M. della Corte anticipated this report by publishing a monograph on the amphitheater in 1930, subsequently revised in a French edition of 1935. And extensive clearing operations directed to the uncovering of long stretches of the city wall, undertaken in the mid-1930's, were fully reported in 1943. Particularly evident in these reports is the tendency to synthesize information, as if the provision of careful descriptions alone were insufficient. That effort of synthesis moved beyond the immediate excavation in order to comprehend larger issues of history, topography, and planning.

When the House of the Surgeon was excavated in 1926—published by Maiuri in the 1930 *Notizie*—it had long been recognized that the building represented an important example of the early Italian atrium house. Trenches were dug in the house and *also* in the street in front in order to expose the stratification of the site and to uncover the foundations; they proved to lie over the foundations of an earlier, pre-Samnite house, somewhat differently arranged. Similar trenches were dug in the "older" sites during the period 1935 to 1941 under or near private houses and public buildings, especially in the Forum area (*Notizie,* 1941). These exploratory trenches produced much information on the building history of the sites examined, the phases of construction, the location of pre-existing structures on the site—not standing in A.D. 79—and the development of the street network. Such stratigraphical researches, using archaeological techniques developed elsewhere, began to illuminate the past of the past in extending the antiquity of Pompeii beyond the horizon of A.D. 79 back into the early sixth century B.C. and even earlier. Two major monographs reflect this new knowledge:

A. Sogliano, *Pompei nel suo sviluppo storico. Pompei preromana (dalle origine all'anno 80 a.C.)*, Rome, 1937; and

A. Maiuri, *L'ultima fase edilizie di Pompei*, Rome, 1942.

Stratigraphical investigations also made possible the scientific analysis of the history of Pompeii's evolution as a city, a topic already broached in 1918 by F. von Duhn who had investigated the stratigraphy of the Triangular Forum twenty years before (*Pompeji, eine hellenistische Stadt in Italien*, Leipzig). The harvest of these explorations into the urban history of Pompeii was reaped by German scholars, interested in the history of Greek and Roman cities and in ancient city-planning. In 1936 F. Noack and K. Lehmann-Hartleben published their seminal study of the Pompeian street system (*Baugeschichtliche Untersuchungen am Stadtrand von Pompeji*, Berlin-Leipzig), followed four years later by A. von Gerkan's solid essay on the plan of Pompeii and its evolution (*Der Stadtplan von Pompeji*, Berlin, 1940). The general history of ancient city-planning was therefore greatly advanced by the modern development of the oldest excavations of ancient Pompeii.

Another avenue of general interest was also explored during this fertile period between the wars. The synthetic analysis of painting had been founded on Mau's systematic arrangement of the fashions of interior decoration into Four Styles. On this basis the Dutch scholar, H. G. Beyen, undertook a thorough investigation of the evolution of Pompeian wall decoration from the Second through the Fourth Style, beginning in 1938 and continuing for three decades. If his classifications became somewhat arbitrary, even finicky, they brought the subtlety of the compositions to light as well as the patterns of change, the latter most important for the history of taste among the Romans. In the 1930's the series, *Monumenti della pittura antica scoperti in Italia*, was launched, insuring the complete publication of entire ensembles of paintings from specified locations, including both decorative schemes and the panel paintings they enframe; for Pompeii, the paintings from the House of the Citharist (1937), the House of M. Fabius Amandio (1938), and the Temple of Isis (1942) were fully published with fine color plates. However useful these studies were—and are—they tended to treat Pompeian painting in isolation, or followed the much older pattern of concentrating on

Excavation work inside the Villa at Oplontis showing the stratification along the walls.

the panel paintings because of their suspected Hellenic content and derivation. In 1929 G. E. Rizzo tried to insert Pompeian painting into a larger historical context by emphasizing the continuity of Hellenistic and Roman painting (*La Pittura ellenistico-romana,* Milan). His interest in the history of style was complementary to L. Curtius' evaluation of the meaning of Pompeian painting in its own context and as a whole, an approach of great value because it addressed both the content of the panel paintings and the decorative ensembles, and their inter-relationships (*Die Wandmalerei Pompejis,* Leipzig, 1929). Curtius influenced C. M. Dawson who investigated the topic of *Romano-Campanian Mythological Landscape Painting* (New Haven, 1944) and isolated several motifs in Pompeian painting whose patterns and meaning were to be distinguished from the sources in Greek art and mythology. Similar thematic studies were undertaken by other scholars of Pompeian painting, often of great value to the history of the Western tradition, such as H. G. Beyen's essay on still-life painting at Pompeii and Herculaneum (1928). Significantly, these studies on planning, urban history, and painting do more than contribute to the growing body of knowledge about Pompeii; they reach out beyond Pompeii to the world at large—to scholars, scientists, and curious persons whose numbers are far greater than in the heyday of Pompeianism.

A Pompeii for the Twenty-Ninth Century

We live in an age of archaeological research; and there never was a time when so much industry and genius were given to restore for the men of today the exact life of our ancestors in the past. All ages, all races, all corners of the planet have been ransacked to yield up their buried memorials of distant times. Rome, Pompeii, Athens, Asia Minor, Egypt, Assyria, India, Mexico, have rewarded the learned digger with priceless relics. The Rosetta stone, the Behistun rock, have revealed entire epochs of civilization to our delighted eyes. We have a passion for *looking backward*—and it is one of our most worthy and most useful pursuits. There is one age, however, for which our archaeological zeal does nothing. We are absorbed in thinking about our ancestors; why do we not give a thought to our descendants? Should we not provide something for posterity? Let us, once in a way, take to *looking forward*; and, with all our archaeological experience and all the resources of science, deliberately prepare a Pompeii, a Karnak, a Hissarlik, for the students of the twenty-ninth century.[4]

252

Garden landscape wall painting located in the cubiculum of the House of the Fruit Orchard.

Rediscovery
As if it were as it was! 1945–1979

AFTER World War II the rebuilding of modern cities took precedence over Pompeii, not only in Italy itself which had suffered severely in the campaigns of 1943–1945 but all over Europe as well. Many cities were so badly damaged that they had to be completely rebuilt, often without reference to their former appearance— Rotterdam, for example. Other cities of greater historical or artistic interest were reconstructed wholly or in part in order to preserve for posterity their former distinctive character—Dresden, Prague, Warsaw, Ancona, the towns along the Arno. Reconstruction of these cities of art and distinguished architecture was not very dependent on the fragmentary rubble left behind after the bombing but relied, instead, on architects' plans and drawings, preserved in archives, photographs, and cityscapes in

Cloudy day overlooking the Villa at Oplontis.

all media, as well as on personal recollections. For the reconstruction of Dresden, the works of Bellotto, an eighteenth-century Italian landscape painter, were essential, since they were both comprehensive and detailed in their depiction of the famous Danubian city. Whatever the source and whatever the pattern of reconstruction and rebuilding, these reborn cities were inhabited, filled with active people, fully engaged in the pleasures and tasks of modern daily life. Not so Pompeii, seen as a mausoleum become a museum, where people once lived but no longer!

Following the War the role of Pompeii as a monument of traditional culture became more complicated, especially in Italy whose resources had been severely extended by the great need to rehabilitate the economic and social structure of the country. As the great economic miracle of post-war Italy began to gather momentum, the national government established the Cassa del Mezzogiorno (the Fund for the South) in order to stimulate economic development in the long depressed areas of the peninsula south of Rome. One line of that development was tourism, a major industry in Italy for centuries; ancient monuments dotted the South and offered a certain attraction for tourists, especially for those bringing hard currency from abroad. Pompeii and other competing archaeological sites were beneficiaries of substantial grants from the Cassa del Mezzogiorno which sought to develop tourism, exploit the archaeological resources of the countryside, and give employment to the many out-of-work southerners, who were largely unskilled laborers. Untrained in the slowly acquired techniques of archaeological excavation and at first without an adequate opportunity to be properly taught—as Spinazzola had trained his work gangs—this labor force at Pompeii was best suited for work on the reconstruction and preservation of previously excavated structures. As a result, in the 1950's and 1960's Pompeii was in the best physical shape it had enjoyed since August 24, A.D. 79 which enhanced its attraction and accessibility to the hordes of tourists who came to visit the handsome ruins.

However, the diverging objectives of tourism and education conflicted in Pompeii over issues of resource allocation. The more funds were devoted to preservation and maintenance, the less there would be available for an active program of excavation, which in turn would itself require expensive conservation of newly found materials and structures. Furthermore, if preservation of the standing monuments became the prime objective, questions were raised about the "what" and "how" of conservation, since as a result of extensive stratigraphical soundings it was increasingly apparent that Pompeii did not possess a single historical identity, but rather several such identities. When it emerged Phoenix-like from the ashes of Vesuvius, Pompeii brought its own past along,

256

An exquisitely-crafted crystal cup in surprisingly good condition found in the excavations in Pompeii.

and part of that past was recoverable, if only sporadically distributed over the town. An analogy can be drawn in this situation to the Forum in Rome which as it now exists has no historical validity because the excavations have exposed elements to the visitor that never would have been visible at any one time in Antiquity; in that sense, the Roman Forum is a monumental collection of different times in one place.

Such treatment did not seem appropriate for Pompeii because so much of it was of one time and place. An attack on the integrity of that situation would impair the site's appeal to the tourist and its special capacity to display the variety of Roman urban life at the fullest. Thus, in the post-war period more funds became available for conservation than for excavation, and the pace of excavation at Pompeii slowed greatly. In addition, the resources of the Cassa del Mezzogiorno were further diluted by application to the more energetic excavation of other Campanian sites, especially Herculaneum, Stabiae, and Torre Annunziata (Oplontis), where local partisans clamored for their proper share of funding, archaeological attention, and tourist income. Unfortunately for Pompeii, in the decade of the 1970's with rapid inflation even the funds for conservation are inadequate with very serious consequences for the preservation of many of the monuments, especially in the older excavations. In the end, neglect may cause more damage to Pompeii than the eruption because should the monuments, once exposed, crumble again into ruin, nothing can restore them, whereas underground they remain safely preserved for the future.

Reacting to the new policies, research projects, undertaken by a large international body of scholars on the evidence already available at Pompeii, led to a flood of special studies, concentrating particularly on the allied fields of urban and social history and on the analysis of programmatic painting (K. Schefold). Exploratory soundings of Pompeian stratigraphy also became more important, since they were relatively inexpensive and addressed directly a major topic of post-war research, the recovery of the pre-Roman past of the town (q.v. A. Maiuri, *Alla ricerca di Pompei preromana*, Naples, 1973). The new dimensions of Pompeii's urban history were effectively displayed in A. W. Van Buren's important review article (Pauly-Wissowa, *RealEncyclopedie* XXI.2, 1952, cc. 1999–2038) which divides the history of the town into ten distinct phases:

1.	Before 700 B.C.	6.	200 to circa 80
2.	700–500	7.	Circa 80–31
3.	Fifth century to circa 424	8.	31 B.C.–A.D. 54
4.	424–250	9.	54–62
5.	250–200	10.	62–79

Wall painting of two ornately decorated pillars and a candelabrum uncovered in the ongoing excavations in the Villa at Oplontis.

259

The "Black Hall" of the House of Fabius Rufus. The three-dimensional
appearance is accentuated by the dark background on which the figures are
painted—among them all the usual favorites: Apollo, Bacchus, Venus and
Leda with her swan.

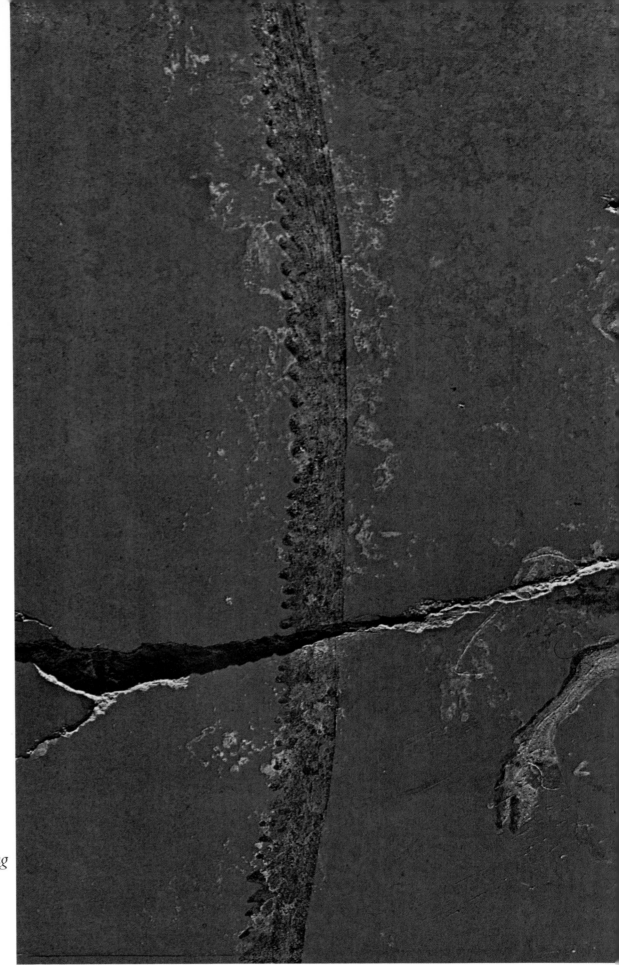

Female figure astride a flying bull, one of the finds in the Villa at Oplontis.

A decorative red ceiling at Oplontis.

A peacock in repose seemingly under the observation of a tragic mask against a columned backdrop, from the new excavations at the Villa at Oplontis.

Wall painting of a bird from the Villa at Oplontis.

These phases can now be distinctly perceived as a result of stratigraphical research over the past fifty years, even if the particular divisions can be questioned. At the same time, the early history of Pompeii has been tied more closely to events and conditions in Campania, Italy, and the Mediterranean world, as they become better known through comparable studies in other archaeologically active sites.

Still, archaeological activity continued positively at Pompeii after 1950 and it may be followed in the *Notizie degli Scavi* (often in arrears), in the *Memorie* and *Rendiconti* of the Accademia Nazionale dei Lincei (Rome), in the *Rendiconti dell'Accademia di Archeologia, Lettere e Belle Arti di Napoli,* in the *Archäologische Anzeiger* published by the German Archaeological Institute in Berlin, in the *Revue Archéologique* (Paris), in the *American Journal of Archaeology*, and since 1975 in the *Cronache Pompeiane*. Scholarly interest in Pompeii, if diffused, has never been greater:

1950

Continuation of excavations in region VIII, especially in insula 5 (baths) and the adjacent house, *House of the Red Walls.* Repair of bomb damage.

Excavations resumed at the great villa at Stabiae (Castellammare) under L. D'Orsi.

Publication of *Pompeiana: Raccolta di studi per il secondo centenario degli scavi di Pompei* (Naples) which reviewed recent achievements and set out future policy.

1951

Additional work on the cavea of the *Large Theater;* continued repair of bomb damage on the *Via dell'Abbondanza.*

1954

Extensive work undertaken on the *Necropolis* outside of the *Nucerian Gate,* indicating a zone of tombs extending back into the pre-Roman period and rivaling the long-known Necropolis outside the Herculaneum Gate. Digging and clearing continued in this area for several years, contributing to the knowledge of Pompeian society as demonstrated by the tombs with their inscriptions. *Tomb of Eumachia,* one of the richest women in Pompeii, discovered.

Section of city wall around the Nucerian Gate and extending to the Amphitheater cleared.

1957

Museo Archeologico Nazionale founded in Naples.

1961

Alfonso de Franciscis made director.

1964

Major stratigraphical sounding in the *Basilica*, complemented in ensuing years by similar work in the *House of the Faun*, the *House of Lucretius Fronto*, the *House of Ceres*, and after 1968 in the *House of C. Julius Polybius.*

1967

Pompeian exhibition opens in Tokyo, Japan.

Decumanus Maximus excavated at Herculaneum.

Excavations begun at the *Villa at Oplontis* (Torre Annunziata); published by A. de Franciscis in 1975.

1968

Consolidation of the *Amphitheater* at Pompeii.

Beginning of excavations on the important *House of C. Julius Polybius* (IX-13-1), restaurateur, on the Via dell'Abbondanza, and continued until *1973*; house is important because of its large peristyle, paintings in the First, Third, and Fourth Styles; elements in its façade dated to the second century B.C., and stratigraphy indicate pre-Roman occupation (A. de Franciscis, *Cronache Pompeiane,* I, 1975). In the summer of *1978* an important deposit of utensils, lamps, and bronze statuary found here, probably buried at the time of the earthquake of A.D. 62.

1970

Work on the Suburban Baths at Herculaneum begun.

Hans Eschebach published his major study of the urban development of Pompeii, *Die stadtbauliche Entwicklung des antiken Pompeji* (Heidelberg); his plan, illustrating the architectural character of Pompeii in A.D. 79, color-coded according to function, has become definitive.

1971

Investigation of the walls intensified, especially at the *Sarno Gate*, cleared by *1972*.

1972

Wilhelmina Jashemski's investigation of Pompeian gardens advanced by discovery of market garden in the *House of the Ship Europa* (I-15-1), identification of plants established by technique adapted from Fiorelli, e.g. pouring plaster into the holes left by the roots (*American Journal of Archaeology* 78, 1974); this discovery complemented her research of the large enclosed orchard of the *House of Octavius Quartio* (II-2-2; formerly known as the House of Loreius Tiburtinus), and the vineyard with related winery in the *Praedia of Julia Felix* (II-4-2) (*American Journal of Archaeology* 77, 1973).

Necropolis outside the Nucerian Gate.

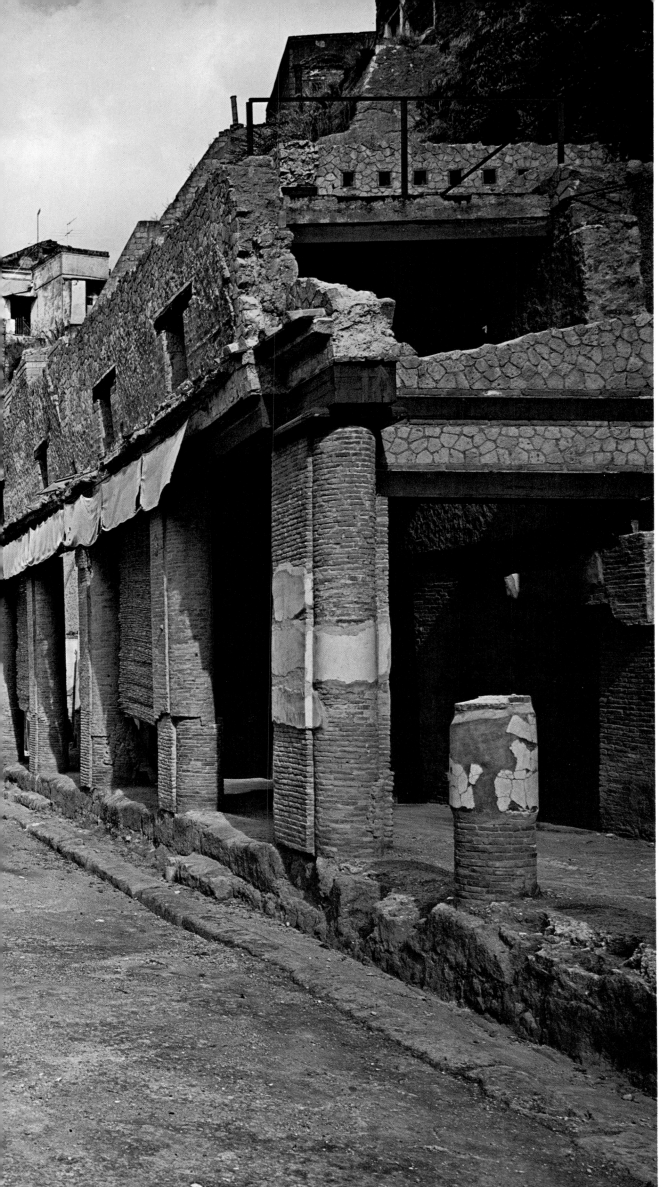

Looking down the broad Decumanus Maximus toward the arched entrance to the Basilica in Herculaneum.

The Collegium of the Augustales, behind the Basilica entrance on the Decumanus Maximus in Herculaneum, dedicated to the Imperial cult; Hercules, Juno and Minerva are pictured on the wall of the alcove.

1973

Exhibition of Life and Art in Pompeii at the Villa Hügel, Essen, Germany; catalogue published under title, *Pompeji, Leben und Kunst in den Vesuvstädten* (Recklinghausen).

1975

First appearance of the *Cronache Pompeiane.*

B. Andreae and H. Kyrielis, editors, *Neue Forschungen in Pompeji* (Recklinghausen), published the papers of the Essen colloquium on Pompeii (1973) including important studies on housing patterns, stratigraphy, gardens, planning, First Style painting, and cults.

Giuseppina Cerulli-Irelli made director.

1976

Discovery of the grave of Marcus Obellius Firmus outside the *Nolan Gate*; his house on the Via Nolana had long been known (IX-10-1.4).

New style guidebook to Pompeii published by F. Coarelli, *Guida archeologica di Pompei* (Verona), complete with up-to-date maps and plans, color photographs, and a valuable introductory essay on the history of Pompeii, on the Pompeians, and on art and architecture.

1977

Pompeian exhibition at the British Museum, London.

1978–79

POMPEII: A.D. 79, Treasures from the National Archaeological Museum, Naples, and the Pompeii Antiquarium, traveling exhibition held at the Museum of Fine Arts, Boston; The Art Institute of Chicago; Dallas Museum of Fine Arts; American Museum of Natural History, New York.

1979

August 24, nineteenth centenary of the destruction of Pompeii.

Other finds, as usual. . . .

Symptomatic of the post-war development of Pompeian archaeology, the major items in its recent history seem to consist largely of publications and exhibitions intended for an international audience and, frequently, compiled by an international body of scholars. Perhaps that is the proper course, demonstrating most effectively the international importance of Pompeii for scholars of antiquity, architects, planners, sociologists, and the general public, but it also indicates the lagging pace of excavation. Leaving so much of Pompeii still buried may hold a treasure for the future, since the constant advance in techniques of excavation and in the analysis of the resulting finds can

Painters' supplies. Full-scale repair jobs were necessary to public buildings and private residences following the devastating earthquake in A.D. 62, and that accounts for the considerable store of supplies that have been discovered within the city. The pigments were mixed with limewater as a binding agent prior to their application to the still-moist plaster on the wall.

Amphorae block the doorway of the House of C. Julius Polybius, one of most important of the newly excavated houses in Pompeii.

well extend and enhance the quality of the archaeological product. These new techniques have already made a creative impression, affecting the field of urban studies and social history and leading to the revision of the general history of Pompeii.

Van Buren's Pompeii article of 1952 (RE XXI.2) reflects an older view of topographical matters with its attention divided between considerations of general layout and the description of the principal building types. The general tenor of his encyclopedic presentation is descriptive rather than analytical, and it is precisely in the latter direction that the most important recent developments in the urban history of Pompeii have

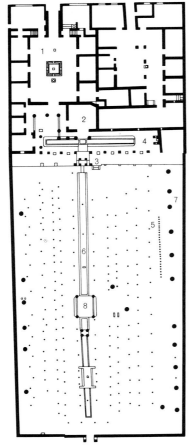

Plan of the House of Loreius Tiburtinus

1. *Atrium*
2. *Oecus*
3. *Peristyle garden terrace*
4. *Open-air dining area*
5. *Line of plants in pots*
6. *Ornamental water channel*
7. *Large trees*
8. *Small pavilion*

Market garden in the House of the Ship Europa

1. *Vegetable gardens*
2. *Path*
3. *Water cistern*

Small dots indicate grapevine roots; black circles indicate roots of various sizes; empty circles indicate plants in pots.

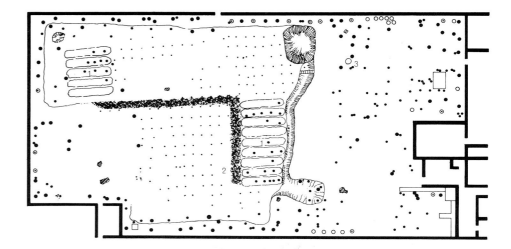

"Cave canem" (beware the dog)—a mosaic menace on the floor of the vestibule in the House of Paquius Proculus (a 1935 Alinari photograph).

Mosaic of doves pulling a pearl necklace out of an ornate gold vase-like vessel, originally located on the floor of an ala(back room) in the House of the Faun.

The Niccolini re-creation of this dove mosaic with its heightened color and meticulous detail catches the imagination—how it must have looked as a decorative floor!

*This so-called "Nile Scene" of water creatures including a crocodile,
hippopotamus and birds was a part of a mosaic floor in the
House of the Faun.*

*Wilhelm Zahn painted this group of floor
mosaic patterns uncovered in Pompeii.*

A two-part mosaic found in an ala (back room) of the House of the Faun.
On the top is a cat with a partridge; below are ducks, fishes and shellfish.
This dual delight was acclaimed when discovered for its delicate execution
and harmonious coloring.

occurred. Eschebach's magisterial study of Pompeii (1970) graphically represents in his now famous plan the functional–architectural structure of the town, broken into the following categories:

1. Public buildings, complexes, squares, baths.
2. Sanctuaries and temples.
3. City services and welfare stations.
4. Dormitories and clubhouses of laborers and artisans.
5. Shops.
6. Inns, restaurants, fast food shops, wineries, taverns, bakeries, gaming houses, and brothels.
7. Private houses used for industrial production.
8. Private housing.
9. Gardens, without peristyles.

As a result of his plotting of the locations of the different functions, it is now possible to analyze the urban structure of Pompeii in many ways:

1. Patterns of distribution become visible.
2. The character and intensity of traffic flow along the major and minor streets can be assessed.
3. Identification of the principal shopping streets or districts is possible.
4. The wealthier and more popular residential districts are more clearly differentiated.
5. Functional changes that occurred in the city as districts or sections of street were altered in character can now be traced historically, with the aid of stratigraphy.
6. The relative population and physical densities of different districts may be evaluated on a more scientific basis.
7. The boundaries of neighborhoods no longer appear to be coterminous with the *insulae*.
8. Relationships between the urban and exurban street network can be more effectively determined.
9. The degree of urban amenity can now be measured in the balance between closed and open spaces, interior and exterior green areas.

The ruins of the Temple of Isis as they appear today.

285

10. The quality of mixed use—mixed zoning in modern terminology—as a fundamental characteristic of Pompeian town life becomes more evident with implications for the social organization of the populace.

Much of this remains to be done, but the foundation for analysis now exists.

One topic has already found its expert. For the past ten years Wilhelmina Jashemski with her team from the University of Maryland has revolutionized our understanding of the Pompeian garden. She has shown the careful mixture of pleasure and profit that property-owners were able to reap from their gardens, and the history of their growth. By recovery techniques analogous to those used by Fiorelli for rescuing the shape of human victims of the eruption, Jashemski has preserved the root system of garden plants, shrubs, and trees, which experts in botany have then been able to identify. By this means the contents of these gardens have been accurately determined, thus contributing greatly to our knowledge of ancient herbiculture and of the Pompeian diet. Furthermore, the greater appreciation of the Pompeian garden as an important urban feature, reinforced by the evidence of large tracts of land under cultivation in the northeast quadrant of town, has led to a reduction in the estimate of population, since it is now understood that Pompeii was not filled up to its walls in A.D. 79.

More and more scholars and archaeologists have turned to the study of those who shaped the ancient city, to the Pompeians themselves, attached to their properties and places of work, busily engaged in "making a living," entertaining themselves at the theater, the amphitheater, in the baths, and with food, drink, and sex, deeply involved in their political, religious, and social groups, studying at school if they were young, decorating their residences and contributing to the beautification of their city, and behaving naturally in those patterns of activity that characterize any human culture. The bibliography on these topics since 1950 has become enormous, ranging from the general evocation of daily life (R. Etienne, *La vie quotidienne à Pompéi,* Paris, 1966) to the analysis of political structure (P. Castrén, "Ordo populusque Pompeianus. Polity and Society in Roman Pompeii," *Acta Inst. Rom. Finland.* 8, 1975) to a near-biography of an important banker, L. Caecilius Jucundus (J. Andreau, "Les affaires de Monsieur Jucundus," *Coll. Ec. Franc.* 19, 1974), whose activities, relatives, and friends were everywhere.

As the people of Pompeii are resurrected from oblivion by scholars who carefully sift through the debris of the past, then Pompeii changes from a City of the Dead to a City of the Once Living, for whom there are no last days.

Requiescat in pace . . .

Epilogue:
What remains to be done?

I. Clear progressively Regions I, IX, III, IV, and V.
II. Excavate the forty percent of Pompeii still buried.
III. Clear the entire extent of the walls.
IV. Investigate the borders of the town to the west.
V. Continue excavation of the exurban streets outside the Gates including the adjacent cemeteries.
VI. Build a new model of Pompeii to replace the nineteenth-century model and maintain its currency in the future.
VII. Build another museum in the western part of town, perhaps directly attuned to the life on the Via dell'Abbondanza.
VIII. Devise new methods of preservation and conservation; investigate Buckminster Fuller's old suggestion of placing a geodesic dome over all or part of Pompeii to protect it from weathering, thus creating a new "Museum with Walls."
IX. Thoroughly reconstruct an insula or two in order to

convey more effectively to the tourist the original appearance of the block as a whole.

X. Continue the work of Tatayana Warsher whose aborted *Codex typographicus pompejanus* (1937) attempted the collection of a photographic album of all Pompeii so far excavated to permit the continued study of the town by scholars everywhere.

XI. Establish an inventory of all works of art, and all objects of any kind, removed from Pompeii since its rediscovery and now located in collections outside of Pompeii.

XII. Attempt to restore the paintings taken from Pompeii and now in the Naples Museum to their original locations, or if that should prove impossible to make exact reproductions of those paintings and reinsert them in standing walls; the same could be done for sculpture and furniture.

XIII. AND . . .

Notes

DISASTER

1. Eugenio Montale, Sarcophagi II from *Ossi di Seppia* (1925), translated by Edwin Morgan, *Poems from Eugenio Montale* (University of Reading, 1959).
2. Pliny, *Letters*, translated by Betty Radice, Loeb Library edition (Cambridge, Mass. and London, 1969), Volume I, pp. 425–435.
3. *Ibid.*, pp. 439–447.
4. Cassius Dio, *Roman History*, translated by E. Cary, Loeb Library edition (Cambridge, Mass. and London, 1961), Volume VIII, pp. 303–309.

DISCOVERY

1. David Mallet, *The Works of David Mallet*, new edition dedicated to William Lord Mansfield (London, 1759), pp. 67, 84–87.
2. The Reverend John C. Eustace, *A Classical Tour through Italy, An. MDCCCII*, sixth edition (London, 1821), Volume 3, pp. 55–56.
3. A. Michaelis, *Ancient Marbles in Great Britain* (Cambridge, 1882), Volume II, p. 737.
4. Friedrich von Schiller, *The Poems of Schiller*, edited and translated by Henry D. Wireman (Philadelphia, 1871).

EXPLOITATION

1. Edward Falkener, *The Museum of Classical Antiquities*, 2nd edition (1860), p. 37. According to E. J. Dwyer's *Pompeian Sculpture in its Domestic Content* (unpublished dissertation, New York University, New York, 1974, p. 11), the *Giornale* makes no mention of any such special arrangement.
2. Sir William Gell and John P. Gandy, *Pompeiana: The Topography, Edifices, and Ornaments of Pompeii* (London, 1832), Volume II, pp. 96–97.
3. J. W. Wall, *Naples and Pompeii* (Burlington Library Co., Burlington, 1856), pp. 12–13.
4. Ferdinand Gregorovius, *The Roman Journals of Ferdinand Gregorovius 1852–1874*, edited by F. Althaus, translated by Mrs. G. W. Hamilton (London, 1907), p. 6.
5. *Arria Marcella*, in the *Complete Works of Théophile Gautier*, translated and edited by S. C. de Sumichrast (London, 1900), Volume VI, pp. 318–320.
6. Mark Twain, *Innocents Abroad* (New York, 1869), Volume II, p. 42.

CLASSIFICATION

1. Lewis R. Farnell, *An Oxonian Looks Back* (London, 1934), p. 174.
2. Malcolm Lowry, "Present Estate of Pompeii" (short story, 1949), *Hear Us O Lord from Heaven Thy Dwelling Place* (New York: J. B. Lippincott, 1961), p. 192.
3. A. W. Van Buren, "Restoring Pompeii," *Archaeology* 6 (1953), pp. 147–148. See also Vittorio Spinazzola, *Pompei alla Luce degli Scavi Nuovi di Via dell'Abbondanza (anni 1910–1923)*, edited posthumously by S. Aurigemma, 3 volumes (Rome, 1953).
4. Frederic Harrison, "A Pompeii for the Twenty-Ninth Century," *Eclectic Magazine of Foreign Literature* (November, 1890), pp. 599–600.

Selected Bibliography

DISASTER and General

Andreae, B. *Pompeji: Leben und Kunst in den Vesuvstädten* [exhibition catalogue, Villa Hügel]. Essen, 1973.

Carrington, R. C. *Pompeii*. Oxford, 1936.

Coarelli, F., ed. *Guida archeologica di Pompei*. Verona, 1976.

Corti, E. C., Conte. *Untergang und Auferstehung von Pompeji und Herculaneum* [with an appendix on recent excavations by T. Kraus]. Munich, 1977.

D'Arms, J. H. *Romans in the Bay of Naples*. Cambridge, Mass., 1970.

Della Corte, M. *Case ed abitanti di Pompei*. Rome, 1954.

Eschebach, Hans. *Pompeji*. Leipzig, 1978.

Etienne, R. *La vie quotidienne à Pompéi*. Paris, 1966.

Grant, M. *Cities of Vesuvius: Pompeii and Herculaneum*. London, 1971.

Leppmann, W. *Pompeii in Fact and Fiction*. London, 1968.

Maiuri, A. "Pompei." *Enciclopedia dell'arte antica*, IV. Rome, 1965, pp. 308–356.

Mau, A. [English translation by F. W. Kelsey]. *Pompeii, Its Life and Art*. New York, 1899.

Pompeiana. Raccolta di studi per il secondo centenario degli scavi di Pompei. Naples, 1950.

Richardson, Lawrence, Jr. "The Libraries of Pompeii." *Archaeology*, 30.6, 1977, pp. 394–402.

Schefold, K. *La peinture pompéienne*. Brussels, 1972.

Tanzer, H. H. *The Common People of Pompeii*. Baltimore, 1939.

Trevelyan, R. *The Shadow of Vesuvius: Pompeii AD 79*. London, 1976.

Van Buren, A. W. *A Companion to the Study of Pompeii and Herculaneum*. 2nd ed. Rome, 1938.

Ward-Perkins, J., and Claridge, A. *Pompeii A.D. 79* [exhibition catalogue]. Museum of Fine Arts, Boston, 1978.

DISCOVERY *(in order of use)*

De Brosses, Charles. *Lettres d'Italie*. 2 vols. Paris, 1928.

————. *Voyage en Italie 1739–1740*. H. Juin ed. Paris, 1964.

Venuti, M. [English translation by W. Skurray]. *A Description of the Ancient City of Heraclea, found near Portici, a Country Palace belonging to the King of the Two Sicilies*. London, 1750.

Macaulay, Rose. *Pleasure of Ruins.* New York, 1953.

Dobai, J. *Die Kunstliteratur des Klassizismus und der Romantik in England.* I. 1700–1750. Bern, 1974, pp. 795–845.

Praz, M. "Herculaneum and European Taste." *Magazine of Art*, 32, 1939, pp. 684–693, 727.

Seznec, J. "Herculaneum and Pompeii in French Literature of the Eighteenth Century." *Archaeology*, 2, 1949, pp. 150–158.

Kimball, F. "The Reception of the Art of Herculaneum in France," in *Studies Presented to D. M. Robinson*, II, 1953, pp. 1254–1256.

———. "The Beginnings of the *Style Pompadour* 1751–1759." *Gazette des Beaux-Arts*, 44, 1944, pp. 58–64.

Cochin, C.-N., and Bellicard, J. C. *Observations sur les antiqués d'Herculanum aujourd'hui Portici.* 2 vols. Paris, 1755.

Jeannerat, C. "Les petits portraits dans le goût pompéien." *Gazette des Beaux-Arts*, 6, 1922, pp. 353–364.

Marechal, P.-S. *Antiquités d'Herculanum ou les plus belles peintures antiques et les marbres, bronzes, meubles, etc., trouvés dans les excavations d'Herculanum, Stabia et Pompeia*, gravées par F. A. David. 12 vols. Paris, 1780–1803.

Schmid, W. "Zur Geschichte der Herkulanischen Studien." *La Parola del Passato*, X, 1955, pp. 478–500.

Hatfield, H. C. *Winckelmann and his German Critics 1755–1781. A Prelude to the Classical Age.* New York, 1943.

Justi, C. *Winckelmann und seine Zeitgenossen.* II, Cologne, 1956, pp. 444–450. III, Cologne, 1956, pp. 445–454.

Pelzel, T. "Winckelmann, Mengs and Canova: A Reappraisal of a Famous Eighteenth-Century Forgery." *Art Bulletin*, 54.3, 1972, pp. 300–315.

Opera di J. J. Winckelmann, Vol. II. Prato, 1831; for his letters on Pompeii and Herculaneum, see also *Werke*, II. Stuttgart, 1847, pp. 135ff., 169ff., 188ff.

Wiebenson, D. *Sources of Greek Revival Architecture.* Pennsylvania State University Press, 1969. Chapter IV, "The Greek-Roman Quarrel," pp. 47–61.

Dobai, J. *Die Kunstliteratur der Klassizismus und der Romantik in England.* II. 1750–1790. Bern, 1975, pp. 476–526, 1191–1230.

Irwin, D. *English Neoclassical Art. Studies in Inspiration and Taste.* Greenwich, CT, 1966, pp. 21–30, 44–75.

Praz, M. [translation by A. Davidson]. *On Neoclassicism.* Northwestern University Press, 1969. Chapter III, "The Antiquities of Herculaneum," pp. 70–90.

Rosenblum, R. *Transformations in Late Eighteenth-Century Art.* Princeton University Press, 1967.

Honour, H. *Neo-classicism.* Penguin Books, Middlesex, 1973. Chapter 2, "The Vision of Antiquity," pp. 43–62.

Mullett, C. F. "Englishmen Discover Herculaneum and Pompeii." *Archaeology*, 10.1, 1957, pp. 31–38.

Vermeule, C. C. *European Art and the Classical Past*. Harvard University Press, 1964, pp. 133ff.

Michaelis, A. *Ancient Marbles in Great Britain*. Cambridge, 1882, pp. 109–113 (on William Hamilton).

Beckford, W. *Dreams, Waking Thoughts and Incidents*. New edition, edited by R. J. Gemmett. Fairleigh Dickinson University Press, 1971, pp. 216–222.

Hibbert, C. *The Grand Tour*. New York, 1969.

Burgess, A., and Haskell, F. *The Age of the Grand Tour*. New York, 1967, pp. 126–128.

Saint-Non, J.-C. de. *Voyage Pittoresque et Description du royaume de Naples et de Sicile*. 4 vols. Paris, 1781–1786.

Goethe, J. W. von. *Italienische Reise*. Edited by H. von Einem. Hamburg, 1951, pp. 198, 199.

Kroenig, W. "L'Eruzione del Vesuvio del 1779 in Hackert, H. Robert, Desprez, Fr. Piranesi, ed altri," in *Scritti in Onore di Roberto Pane*, Istituto di Storia dell'Architettura dell'Università di Napoli, 1972, pp. 423–442.

Chateaubriand, F. R., Vicomte de. *Voyage en Italie*. Edited by J.-M. Gautier. Geneva, 1968, pp. 104, 105, 108ff., 119–122.

Leitzmann, A. "Die Quellen von Schillers 'Pompeji und Herkulanum'." *Euphorion*, 12, 1905, pp. 557–561.

Von Hagen, Benno. "Pompeji im Leben und Schaffen Goethes." *Goethe*. Viermonatsschrift der Goethe-Gesellschaft. Neue Folge des Jahrbuchs, Jahresheft, 1944, pp. 88–108.

Werner, P. *Pompeji und die Wanddekoration der Goethezeit*. Munich, 1970.

Birchall, A. "The Story of Colossus." *Illustrated London News*, Sept. 1978, pp. 71–75.

Kelder, Diane. *Aspects of "Official" Painting and Philosophic Art 1789–1799*. Garland, New York, 1976, pp. 1–48.

EXPLOITATION *(in order of use and not previously mentioned)*

Dobai, J. *Die Kunstliteratur des Klassizismus und der Romantik in England*. III. 1790–1840. Bern, 1977, pp. 603ff., 620ff., 1216ff.

Clay, E., and Frederickson, M. *Sir William Gell in Italy: Letters to the Society of Dilettanti 1831–1835*. London, 1976.

De Jorio, A. *Plan de Pompéi et remarques sur les edifices*. Naples, 1828.

————. *Guida di Pompei*. Naples, 1836.

Dahl, C. "Recreators of Pompeii." *Archaeology*, 9.3, 1956, pp. 182–191.

Pompeii, as Source and Inspiration: Reflections in Eighteenth- and Nineteenth-Century Art [exhibition catalogue]. University of Michigan Museum of Art, Ann Arbor, 1977.

Börsch-Supan, Eva. *Die Kataloge der Berliner Akademie-Kunstsammlungen 1786–1850.* 3 vols. Berlin, 1971, catalogue numbers 452–457, 472–483, 1292, 1293, 1451, 1452, 1453, 1465.

——. *Garten-, Landschafts- und Paradeismotive im Innenraum.* Berlin, 1968, p. 471, number 2047.

Roux, H., and Barré, L. *Herculanum et Pompéi.* 8 vols. Paris, 1841; (on the paintings, bronzes, and mosaics from these sites in Naples; frequently reprinted and translated).

Scharf, G. *London—Crystal Palace. The Pompeian Court.* London, 1854.

Dejean de la Batie, M.-C. "La Maison Pompéienne du Prince Napoléon Avenue Montaigne." *Gazette des Beaux-Arts*, 137, 1976, pp. 127–134.

Neuerburg, Norman. "The New J. Paul Getty Museum." *Archaeology*, 27.3, July 1974, pp. 175–181.

Cayla, A. "La 'Maison Pompéienne' construite par Alfred Normand en 1860." Académie des Beaux-Arts, 1957/58, pp. 61–65.

Gautier, T.; Houssaye, A.; and Coligny, C. *Le Palais Pompéien de l'Avenue Montaigne. Etudes sur la Maison Greco-Romaine. Ancienne residence du Prince Napoléon.* Paris, 1866.

The Second Empire 1852–1870. Art in France under Napoleon III [exhibition catalogue]. Philadelphia Museum of Art, 1978, catalogue numbers VI–12 (Boulanger painting of the Maison Pompéienne), VI–22 (Chassériau's painting of a *tepidarium* at Pompeii), VI–37 (Paul-Alfred de Curzon's "A Dream in the Ruins of Pompeii"), I–22 (drawing by Normand for the Maison), and I–9 (watercolor by Jacques-Felix Duban of a Pompeian architectural fantasy).

Jammes, A., et al. *Alfred-Nicolas Normand, architecte; photographies de 1851–1852* [exhibition catalogue]. Paris, 1977/78.

Van Zanten, D. *The Architectural Polychromy of the 1830's.* Garland, New York, 1977, pp. 36–41.

Amaya, M. "The Roman World of Alma-Tadema." *Apollo*, Dec. 1962, pp. 771–778.

Swanson, V. G. *Alma-Tadema, The Painter of the Victorian Vision of the Ancient World.* New York, 1977.

Gregorovius, F. *Euphorion. Eine Dichtung aus Pompeji in vier Gesangen.* Leipzig, 1883.

Wickert, L. *Theodor Mommsen. Eine Biographie*, II. Frankfurt, 1964, pp. 179–180.

McMahon, Anna B., editor. *With Shelley in Italy.* Chicago, 1905, pp. 187–195.

Giannone, P. *Le ruine di Pompei. Saggio poetico.* Naples, 1827.

Murphy, Alexandra R. *Visions of Vesuvius* [exhibition catalogue]. Museum of Fine Arts, Boston, 1978.

Bianche, G. *Una notte sulla rovine di Pompei. Romanzo storico.* Naples, 1833.

Zipser, R. A. *Edward Bulwer-Lytton and Germany.* Bern/Frankfurt, 1974.

Gerdts, W. H. *American Neo-Classic Sculpture.* New York, 1973, pp. 120, 121 (on Rogers' "Nydia").

Lemercier, A. *Les derniers jours de Pompéi; imité de Bulwer.* Tours, 1842.

Kaden, W. "Scenen römischen Lebens in Pompeji." *Über Land und Meer. Allgemeine Illustrierte Zeitung,* no. 37, 1884, pp. 750–751, ills. pp. 740–741.

Rhode, Eric. "The Outline of a Couch." A review of *Berggasse 19, Sigmund Freud's Home and Offices, Vienna, 1938. The Photographs of Edmund Engelmann* (Basic Books, 1978); and *Sigmund Freud, His Life in Pictures and Words.* Ernst Freud, Lucie Freud, and Ilse Grubrich-Simitis, editors (André Deutsch: London, 1978); in *The Times Literary Supplement,* Nov. 24, 1978, p. 1355.

CLASSIFICATION *(in order of use and not previously mentioned)*

Lingg, H. *Ausgewählte Gedichte.* Edited by P. Hense. Stuttgart/Berlin, 1905.

Fawcett, E. "Pompeii." *Cosmopolitan,* 24, Nov. 1897–April 1898, p. 182.

Müller, W. A. "Die archäologische Dichtung in ihrem Umfang und Gehalt." *Königsberger Deutsche Forschungen,* Hft. 3, 1928, pp. 1–84, pp. 7– 21 (on Pompeii).

Michaelis, A. *A Century of Archaeological Discoveries.* New York, 1908.

Daniel, G. E. *A Hundred Years of Archaeology.* London, 1950.

Hanotaux, G. *Les villes retrouvées. Thebes d'Egypte. Ninive. Babylone. Troie. Carthage. Pompéi. Herculanum.* 2nd edition. Paris, 1885.

Lessing, J., and Mau, A. *Wand- und Deckenschmuck eines römischen Hauses aus der Zeit des Augustus.* Berlin, 1891, p. 1.

REDISCOVERY *(in order of use and not previously mentioned)*

Ciprotti, P. "Rassegna bibliografica pompeiana, 1946–1955." *Studia et documenta historiae et Juris,* 21, 1955, pp. 409–427.

De Franciscis, A. *The Pompeian wall paintings in the Roman Villa of Oplontis.* Recklinghausen, 1975.

Bibliographical note: Whatever is cited in the text is not cited here.

List of Illustrations and Photographic Credits

297

298

Index

303

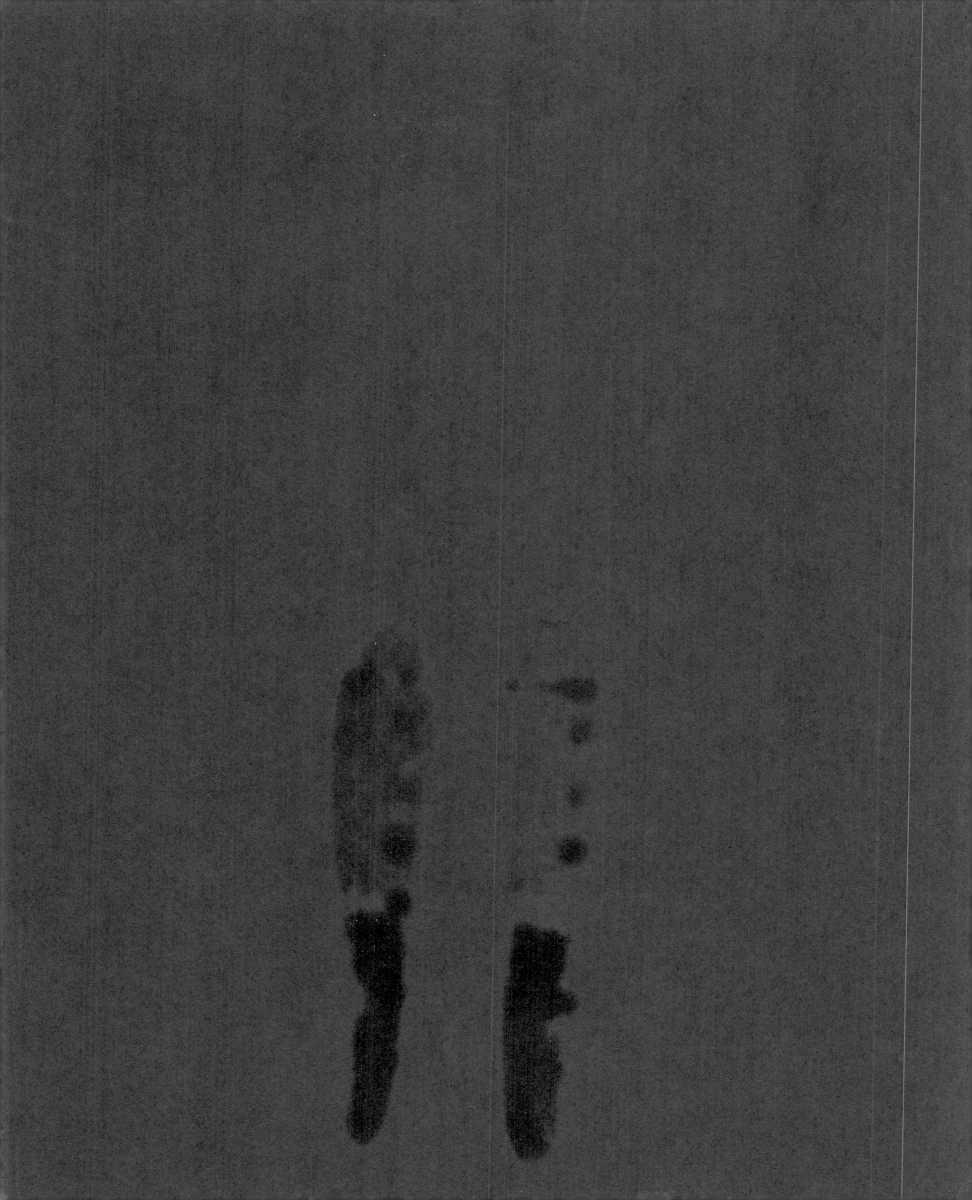